Félix Vallotton, *Ex Libris L. Joly*

# Purr and Yowl

3-23-24

# Purr *and* Yowl

## AN ANTHOLOGY OF POETRY
## ABOUT CATS

*to Tee —
with gratitude
and best wishes!*

### EDITED BY
### DAVID D. HOROWITZ

*David D. Horowitz*

World Enough
Writers

ISBN: 978-1-936657-93-3

Cover art: *Wisdom and Wildness* by Deborah DeWit
Pastel, 20"x30", 2006.
Huckleberry Farms Studios: https://deborahdewit.com/

Editor Photo: Jan Nicosia

Designed by Tonya Namura using Times New Roman and Dream Big

For information, please contact the publisher:

**World Enough Writers**
c/o Concrete Wolf
PO Box 2220
Newport, OR 97365-0163

Email: WorldEnoughWriters@gmail.com

Website: https://worldenoughwriters.com

*for cats*

*and people who appreciate them*

*There are two means of refuge from the miseries of life: music and cats.*
—Albert Schweitzer

*Time spent with cats is never wasted.*
—Sigmund Freud

Henriëtte Ronner-Knip, *en her Katjes*

## EDITOR'S NOTE

Cats lick, nuzzle, play, slink, hunt, purr, and yowl, and millions of people are fascinated by them. Among those millions are the poets who contributed work to this anthology. No matter what their gender, orientation, ethnic background, or political and religious views, these poets share a fascination with cats—and despite sometimes bewildering or frustrating us humans, felines provide us pleasure, love, and purpose. So, bless cats. Hooray for cats! And thank you to this anthology's poets for describing and celebrating them in so many different, engaging ways.

David D. Horowitz, Editor
Seattle, 2023

Jean Bernard Duvivier, *Liggende kat*

# CONTENTS

# Purr and Yowl

Pierre-Auguste Renoir, *Woman with a Cat*

*Gail White*

## CAT SPOTTING

I have been one acquainted with the cats.
I know the twistings of their crooked hearts,
the music of their mews, the sharps and flats,
the way one cat can play a hundred parts,
mother and child, dancer and acrobat,
a loving mistress in a new mink stole,
a dominatrix whose imperious pat
can leave a scar, a healer of the soul.
All these and more in one neat package blend,
ready to claim a lap, a hand, an arm,
because they know we're helpless in the end,
addicted to their soft, self-centered charm,
like chocolate creams and butter-laden fats.
I have been one acquainted with the cats.

*Gail White*

## FAT CAT

My cat, no Lassie, looks at me
with eyes whose green tranquility
could watch me drown as long as she
had just been fed. She ought to be
a grand Episcopalian cat
with bluejay feathers on her hat,
who flips her furs across the pew,
complacently ignoring you.
A cat who gets her every wish,
who knows what wine to have with fish,
imposingly, serenely fat,
a white-gloved Southern Lady cat.

For cats who have a sense of worth,
there is no higher form of birth.
We rather may anticipate
to reach the nobler feline state
where fame and wealth are trivial things,
to purr on Popes and shed on kings.

*Gail White*

## THE SOLITARY WOMAN

In a tiny cottage called The Laurel Tree
the woman lived alone. Nobody came
to see her and she had no family,
so week by week her life was much the same.
She went to church and said the rosary,
took in the mail for neighbors out of town,
adopted cats, caught news on BBC,
and at a roll-top desk she wrote things down—
things no one ever saw, although we guessed
a novel, memoirs, poetry, and more—
but we saw nothing, though we did our best.
And when she died alone, at eighty-four,
with no companion but a big gray cat,
we pitied her. We were such fools as that.

Henriëtte Ronner-Knip, *St. Nicholas series*

*Gail White*

## CAT HOARDER

My children think I have too many cats.
I don't agree, but I know what it means.
They think I'm getting senile, breeding bats
in this old belfry. Children don't know beans.
Wait till they're old and see their crepey skin
like washed unironed taffeta, their veins
a railway map of Europe, while they spin
unheard-of nightmares in diminished brains.
Before your body is a nuisance more
than a delight, before you'd welcome death
sooner than one more catheter, before
June weather chills you with December's breath
and your unlovely skin needs warmer furs,
my dears, you'll love what sits on you and purrs.

*Gail White*

## WHY CATS KEEP TURNING UP IN MY WORK

Cats blink at dogs of little wit
who fawn and flutter round their master,
aware their own aloofness bit
gets what they want and gets it faster.

A cat survives on brain and nerve;
its feral life is fierce and fecund,
and yet its dignified reserve
makes Greta Garbo come in second.

Although their servants may be slow
and need to be discreetly prodded,
cats never beg, because they know
that once in Egypt they were godded.

As such their images are used
in sinewed line and sinuous rhythm.
In sport they keep the Muse amused,
and even in sleep the Force is with them.

*Gail White*

## ABELARD, OR LOVE GONE WRONG

My altered cat runs out the door
and rackets round the yard.
Because he'll be a stud no more,
I call him Abelard.

But when he meets a lady cat
with soft and yielding paws,
he doesn't quite remember that
he's not the man he was.

He climbs her back and bites her neck—
he recollects the game.
But still he meets a fatal check:
results are not the same.

(How often, when romances end,
it puzzles cats and men
to know why last night's lady friend
will not step out again.)

Now other cats, with raucous glee,
cry out their mating song,
while Abelard sits home with me
and wonders what went wrong.

*Gail White*

## SAINT FRANCIS PREACHES TO THE CATS, WHO PAY NO ATTENTION

You cats and kittens, praise the Lord
who gave you claws to be your sword,
who clothed you with his softest fur
and graced you with your gracious purr.

He made you hunters without peer,
attentive both in eye and ear.
But when you take your prey alive,
be merciful—spare one in five.

They listened, but with hearts reserved.
They thought his praises well deserved.
But when he turned to good advice,
their eyelids fell. They dreamed of mice.

*Gail White*

## THE MUEZZIN

My cat awakens me to say
(while giving me her nose to kiss)
That nothing else I do today
Will be as just as this.

To feed God's creatures everywhere
(but chiefly those within my keep)
Is my sufficient morning prayer,
And better far than sleep.

*Gail White*

## OBSEQUIES OF AN EGYPTIAN CAT

Bastet, cat-headed deity, hear!
You that are the gentle heat of the sun,
Remember the warmth of little Menhet.
You that pounce and slay the Serpent of Darkness,
Remember this small but mighty hunter.
She curled in a perfect circle like the sun
And her eyes changed with the phases of the moon.
Evil in the form of a Rat
was slain by her claws.
Now she faces a long journey
And the way is dark.
Place her gently in the boat of Osiris.
She is small and will take up little room.

*Jack Harvey*

## CATS

Cats' philosophy.

Stay close to home.

Avoid people with
cold hands;

in plain sight
hide all the time.

Walk alone.

Live at night.

Trust the moon.

Richard Wakefield

## CONTEMPLATION

The cat wakes up to see the spot of sun
that she's been basking in has eased away
across the kitchen floor, as it has done
a dozen times this silent winter day.
She contemplates the light from where she lies
as if she's weighing whether to remain
or if the work it takes to stretch, to rise,
to move is worth whatever warmth she'll gain.
And move she does, at last, to curl once more
upon the cat-sized circle, settled in
as if her little weight upon the floor
could pin the sun, could stop the planet's spin.
I'm chilled to think a prayer is but a plea
that God might deign to stop this whirling sphere,
to rearrange the universe for me
that I might have a moment's comfort here.
Then quietly, so not to wake the cat,
I rise and stretch, adjust the thermostat.

*Timothy Steele*

## FOR KASHMIR

Sooner or later in the night,
He'd spring onto the bed,
Advance along my flank, and curl
And settle by my head.
I'd stroke his coat to welcome him,
Amused that he should treat
The hive of human intellect
As just a source of heat.

Yet on his last trip to the vet,
He knew I was distressed.
He buried, as I cradled him,
His head against my chest,
And, on my shoulder, placed a paw
And seemed, though drained, to be
Making an ultimate, resigned
Attempt to comfort me.

After his death, I told myself
His was a lucky life.
A starving and flea-ridden stray,
He found me and my wife
And lived with us some sixteen years:
Millions of felines fare
Far worse and never have a chance
Of knowing love or care.

Still, sometimes, waking in the night,
I miss him, and I nurse
The hope that, in the Consciousness
Which dreams the universe

And comprehends all that occurs,
We sleep and wake together
As we did in this lifetime, brow
To brow, nose to nose leather.

*Timothy Steele*

# THE MOUNTAIN LION OF
# CENTRAL PARK

*—Edward Kemeys's sculpture* Still Hunt

He crouches on a ledge above East Drive;
Ivy half hides him from potential prey.
Though attributes that helped his forbears thrive
Don't suit the wildernesses of today,
Readers and sunbathers on nearby lawns
And joggers slowing to a winded trudge
Up Cedar Hill are lucky that he's bronze
And, while appearing ravenous, can't budge.

A self-sufficient, old-school predator,
Straightforward in his stealth, he must despise
Those who, when hungry, visit food trucks for
A taco or a burger and some fries;
Must cringe at us poor strollers, so bereft
Of courage that we yelp when, like a shot,
Cyclists flash past us, crying "On your left!"
Less as a warning than an afterthought.

Despite his baleful air, he's popular.
Tourists who otherwise have overdosed
On landmarks shoot him with their phones and share
His image via email or a post.
School kids on field trips stop and pay him court;
One draws him now, her sketchpad set (for lack
Of any better surface or support)
On a bent-slightly-forward classmate's back.

Such tributes cannot balance the accounts
Between him and our species. We are legion:
We extirpated living catamounts
And our own native brethren from this region.
The park refreshes us. We can, from here,
Walk to the Frick, the Met, the Guggenheim.
But our convenience renders him a mere
Symbol of the Indigenous Sublime.

Most are too rushed to buck the status quo
Or question how we've gotten where we are.
Yet some who pass the great cat, as they go
Between the Boathouse and the Reservoir,
May mutely apologize for what the Dutch
And later civilized barbarians seized.
He glares out toward Fifth Avenue, not much
Concerned with guilt, and not the least appeased.

William Dunlop

## OLD TOM

First—just a kit—a boot squelched him,
voided his screeching innards.
Then a charged flex had him reeling,
salted his whiskers
with a fizzy icing.

Once he was drowned
though he scrabbled his ratty scrawn
out of the rainbutt, polished it off
licking the rest of his lives into shape.
Once he was stoned

by dead-end kids ganged for a killing:
he laid down his ears and scarpered
like a wink of spit off a shovel,
and counted his breaks on the rooftop.
Next, he took poison

neat from the garbage's delicatessen:
by jerks, he coughed up a lifetime
of hairballs and rotgut gobbets.
Once a tussle of yipsnapper mongrels
had him worried to death.

Once he was hanged if the clinching crook of a tree
couldn't bear him to cling to his freezing.
And once, in a yowling rut up the alley,
sharpslashers nailed him, scraped on his throatstrings,
clipped off an ear by their scoring.

Now he considers chances,
thinning his longshot eyes, switching
a nibble of tail at the odds.
He reckons his claws in, and purrs: eight down,
the hell of a tough one to go.

*William Dunlop*

## THE LION'S SHARE

The bars, being there, slice lions down to size:
this one was mighty brave to take the air
of wintry London; glum, he stood
regardant on his skimpy field of mud,
and suffered our clear stare
with a prim wincing of uncivil eyes.

We looked around him, smug, and almost bored
by weight of haunch and shoulder, lean
intake of loin, the paws' disarming pudge.
His jaw's hard slant, the bitter lemon wedge
of face seemed merely mean,
seedy, familiar. Till he roared.

Not in grand rage, not raw magniloquence
of appetite; more in the passive voice
of utter boredom: *God, I've been mucked enough,*
said his large grumble as the grudging cough
lurched out of him. And blew the bars
apart, that instant, screamed our common sense

of hearing, in recoil. Not mere loud sound,
the living voice is fleshing-out of breath.
We felt his press on us, the crisp of hair
scorched by his rancor sulphuring the air—
no breathing-space with death
one leap away—and then our weak eyes found
(the bars being there) they were just looking round.

*Jean Syed*

## THE CAT AND THE LION

I have a magnificent lion—
On a Persian rug it sits,
Being stuffed and no scion
Of snarling vertebrates.

When my son paid his overdue call,
His cat visited too
But wouldn't get out from her hold-all:
A frozen, scared statue.

Yet when he stroked the lion's ear
She looked on him with awe
And emerged trustfully, no fear,
With clipped claws nudged its paw.

*Diane Webster*

## LICK OF WIND

Two lion sculptures guard
the entrance, so if you're
frightened by one and back away
toward the other,
you never pass between them
and the entrance remains a façade.

Two lion sculptures guard
the entrance; I see only
kitties, and pet one's foot.
Not wanting to favor one
over the other, I pet
the back of the other.

Two lion sculptures
bask in sunshine.
I pat each of them
as I leave.
Is that a purr
I hear on the lick
of wind around my ears?

*Victoria Ford*

## THE CARACAL

A large cat, whose larger eyes
pierce the skin of sight,
the caracal by name is called
"black ear," as though that tuft, that hair
shadowing it from sound,
solos nearer truth
than do sensations equally acute,
for how can ears endure
what eyes dissect in every shade?
Even with a sympathy
walled into the public zoo,
were this lynx to hear
the structures of our guilt and fear
what defense could it erect
against a doubled sense of cage?
There is a tuft of durability
in all who live, collars turned up
against the gnashing of wind,
hands glassed in from the mangled
squirrel against the road,
a configuration of voice
howling against the visible
entombment of a living thing.

_David Denny_

## SUBURBAN SCENE

The mountain lion sleeps in the sycamore.
He is first spotted by the jogger, who calls
the sheriff, who calls the game warden.
They stand now at a safe distance while
the animal twitches and the great black-tipped
tail sweeps. He is stretched out across
a heavy horizontal branch where trail turns
sidewalk. Nearby a plaque lists the names
of the city council who sanctioned this paving.

Cars slow. Neighbors gather and whisper.
No one asks what has brought the creature
down into the land of poodles and dachshunds,
to the level ground of trash trucks and school
buses, backpacks and briefcases. Like the
skinny deer who come to sip at the creek,
the drought has drawn him down from the hills.

The warden considers his options. 180 pounds,
he guesses, of tawny muscle and claws and jaws.
When he awakens it will be to prowl and stalk
and devour. The cop thinks of his two-year-old
standing naked in the kiddie pool. The neighbors
notice the strong musky tang, how it lingers
in the absence of breeze. How long has this
beast been snoozing among us? What havoc
will awaken when he springs to the ground?

The warden slides a tranquilizer dart into
his rifle. The cop cracks open his shotgun
and loads both barrels. The neighbors take

another step back from the caution tape,
point their camera phones as the lion stirs,
yawns, stretches. Dusk soon. The cool
darkness calls. His yellow eyes blink open,
survey the hunting ground, rich with prey.

*David Denny*

## FLEA MEDS

Once a month he stalks his cat,
sneaks up on her from behind.

It's the only way to get it done.
He pins her head and hips,

parts the fur on the back
of her neck, squeezes

the tiny tube, releasing
the foul-smelling gel

to her skin. She yowls
at him, turning, and leaps

for the gap in the sliding
glass door. It'll be midnight

before she returns,
curling at his feet,

her tail whipping
against him, the oily spot

on her neck a mark of
her shame, his betrayal.

*Holly J. Hughes*

## MORNING WALK AFTER READING
## THE SUTRAS

My cat doesn't read the sutras, doesn't know
she's violating a precept, knows only that the squirrels
chatter in the trees and if she can catch one,

she will. Right now, she has a Douglas squirrel
in her mouth. *Drop that squirrel*, I shout, even
though it's 7 am. I gather him up; he fits in my palm,

curled, eyes widening as he takes each breath,
mouth open. *Please keep breathing*, I ask whoever's
in charge of squirrels' lives, though flecks of red

blossom around matchstick yellow teeth as he sighs,
blinks, shutters his eyes. Not ready to give up,
I lay him on a scrap of blue flannel in a box,

fill a saucer with water, place him high on a shelf
in the woodshed, set out on my walk. I've gone
just two blocks when my dog re-appears,

neighbor's cat like a fur muff in his mouth.
My dog doesn't read the sutras either, but knows
 it's wrong to chase cats. *Drop that cat*, I shout,

He drops the cat, feigns innocence, grins, tongue
lolling, wants only a biscuit, then to walk again.
Where's the lesson in this? The cat lived, the squirrel

will not, and neither my dog nor cat are worried
about enlightenment or the afterlife. In the meantime,
we walk the road together: dog, cat, spirit of the squirrel

dying in his cardboard box and me, wanting a sign
that someone does have their eye on the sparrow,
on all of us—the squirrel, the cat, the dog, and me.

*Holly J. Hughes*

## SOPHIE CALLED OUT BY THE MOON

Tonight, the gibbous moon rises late,
calls you from a warm bed to roam
moon-drenched grasses for mice,

voles, all the small creatures that scurry
in the dark, now lit by the restless moon
on her sweep across the sky. Waking

in the night, I see you're gone, go to
the door to call you home, my voice
echoing into a night not empty.

When you return, it's as if from
a great distance, dutifully, annoyed,
calling out in response—*enough! I'm coming—*

to be held and petted, staying only
long enough to reassure me
you're still with us, then with a *flipflap*

of the cat door, you're out again to wade
vast puddles of moonlight, sure-footed
in your need for wildness, returning

hours later to pad silently up the stairs,
climb into your nest in the pile of covers.
Only then will you greet me, bat my hand,

one claw extended as if to remind me
that if you wanted, you could shred it.
Instead, you circle once, twice, drop

down, tuck your sweet, murderous
face under your tail, sink into dreams
of endless, moonlit fields of mice.

*Holly J. Hughes*

## SOPHIE'S LAST STAND

She's losing her fur in clumps,
resembles a moth-eaten sweater,

even the tips of her ears droop
like tired flags on a windless day.

And for days now, her pink tongue
has lapped only chicken broth,

and though she hasn't budged from
her bed on the chair, a gray comma,

the small engine of her heart still
chugs on like a motorboat, purring

as I pace and fret, wonder how many
days, hours, minutes she has left.

*That's it*, I think, and just
as I'm calling the vet, she leaps

onto the old oak table, sinks
into her familiar crouch. I look up;

*how can it be?* She's stalking
a junco, outside at the feeder.

Motionless, tail twitching,
*domesticated* a word

she never agreed to learn—
and why should she,

a cat to her last, fierce breath.

*Joseph Powell*

## ORIANA

As beautiful as her name—
Himalayan/Siamese—
eyes bluer than chicory blossoms,
beige and brown fur as soft as a mink's pelt.

She had her race's aloof disdain
for affection, also beauty's regal comportment
as if owed something,
had some bestowed secret promise.

Her sport was mainly us—
she'd face a wall and do flips
until she tired of our watching.
If we left for a weekend
she'd disappear for days.
With revenge cool and coy,
she finally came to her called name.
She dismissed the scratch pads
and ruined two couches by honing her nails
for the outside world.

She made her own cat-door
through the study's window screen,
made a new one as each was replaced.
She came and went at night
bringing in dead baby rabbits,
dropping them on the laundry floor,
half-living mice, a rat.
Was it her prowess
or our excited revulsion she enjoyed?

When the window was closed
she'd lay her trophy on the Welcome mat
and cry until we saw her prize—
how like our own vanity,
our show-and-tell, our medals on lapels,
our bumptious hats.

When she left the comforts of the house,
she'd enter the farm world of coyotes,
bobcats, horned owls, cougars…
enter a survivor's alertness
she maintained for seventeen years.
When her heart gave out,
like her namesake, that magician in *Dinotopia*,
her final performance was disappearing
inside us, this ink.

*Joseph Powell*

## SCROLLING FACEBOOK:
## THE BIG CATS

I admit to watching animals, not people,
perhaps because they haven't learned to pose.
The big cats whose eyes and pacing claws
were chilling beasts of marauding muscle
now seem but cruelly evolved to risk their shadows
at every meal. A buffalo's horn breaks a jaw;

a submerged croc can vise their drinking faces;
a pissed wildebeest saves his brother and launches
the lion's body unawares; a giraffe's kick
can crack a skull, a leg, or knock him nameless.
They're doomed to eat this living meat for lunch.
Hyenas and dogs attack to steal a snack.

One wonders why they post these killing scenes—
to educate my fears and provoke a sympathy?
to suggest we are nature's cats without the risk?
to brag about their safari's footage, their means?
to say how fluently death stalks each passerby?
how quickly our stars can fall to an asterisk?

Injured, they suffer a coward's crawling death.
Of course, one feels the victim's bloody plight—
the cat's pounce, the tearing claws, and terror's eyes
when innocent pleasure—a drink or sex's date—
becomes but death's foreplay, its searchlight.
Our cameras catch the smallest quiver and cry.

Why do we watch? Is it the armchair thrill
of drama not our own, to vaguely feel
the pulse of nature, its predatory zeal?

We learn how thoroughly we've conquered safety,
how easily we breathe in our certainty,
how fierce and red is the underside of beauty.

They don't regret the calf or fawn they ate,
full-bellied sleep is how they celebrate.
These majestic cats have private, interior
lives that sun and sport—boring behavior
the camera doesn't spend a minute on.
Awake or asleep, their leap is their horizon.

*Michael Fraley*

## THE OLD LION

The lion holds a special place
Of honor in the scheme of things;
His fearless presence clearly brings

A noble air to what was base.
And more than this, a pleasing fright—
Such untamed danger stirs delight.

Compelling to his very core,
We celebrate the thrill of raw
Emotion stirred by tooth and claw.

His roar will certainly restore
The primal self that lurks below
Our modern world of self-made woe.

Though for his fierceness he is feared,
The lion is by all revered.
A judge's eye, a king's command,
His bearing is both proud and grand.

*Michael Fraley*

## THE CAT

—*for Janine the Queen*

With slipstream ease, she moves the same
As wind and water smoothly play
Around whatever blocks their way.

Her nature is not wholly tame;
With deadly skill, she stalks her prey—
The fearful mouse, the bird at play.

The art of grooming brings her fame;
A tongue of pink beyond compare
Transforms her fur with utmost care.

As active as she is, she still
Finds time each day, surprisingly,
For sleeping quite contentedly.

Mealtime provides a special thrill
When she approves the choice we've made;
She's quick to judge what makes the grade.

The cat is independent, true,
So *very highly favored* you
Will feel when she selects your lap
To curl up in and take a nap.

J.K. Hayward-Trout

## EMPTY CHAIR

Tiffany lamp glows,
Casting a single spotlight
On an empty stage,
Catching the sheen of fabric
And piles of abandoned fur.
She had claimed her bed long ago.
The one in the living room
With the open arms and soft belly.
Now a living shrine.

At times when she asked, I was the chair,
The open arms and warm cushion.
I miss her curled or sprawled,
Her paw to my chest
When she needed to know,
Or prove she was mine or, I was hers.

I never went chasing affection.
She was in-charge of her love,
Not me.

Today, forgetting, I went looking
Then remembered,
She has long lived in another place.
I imagine her.
Still living.
Just not with me.

*J.K. Hayward-Trout*

## THE RESCUE

I ponder her given name: Mona? Mona Lisa?
Calling her Tinker-Bella then Bella Luna.
She approves with a silent pounce.
Her gentle slow blinking stare.
Rattling purr, she bows against me.
Shares my wonder of indoor things.
Stalking gnats, or spidery prey.
She reminds me to look outside
At the bird, the lizard, a frog.
And after distraction's played
We smile, heavy lidded, a deep breath release.
The plush warmth of her nest—my lap.
I forgive her everything,
Midnight zoomies, smashing butter dish, stealing sleep.
She gives me contention,
But I am content.
I am rescued.

*Joanne Clarkson*

## LUCKY

They needed to save something so they
adopted a cat. Not knowing cats
don't need any salvation except
themselves. They expected gratitude
of soft vibrations. The adoration
of kind green eyes. They got
a yowl at 3 a.m. every damn night,
moon or no moon. They received
a scratch on the back of unrequested
touch. The arrogant animal turned
its rump to any food except real tuna.
It did use the litter box and groom itself
to royalty. It could leap five feet
to capture a fly and chase a laser beam
for hours. And on nights with the most
ghosts, it slept pressed close
against an invisible sadness. They went from
telling friends they rescued an abandoned
feline to describing how she saved them,
two people who didn't know
they were lonely or realize they were lost.

*Laura J. Bobrow*

## HOMAGE TO JUSTINE

Dear tawny cat with startling amber eyes,
bewitching cat with unmatched booted paws
forever tangled up in ribbon ties,
although your whiskers quiver straight as straws
you did not earn your name *Justine* because
your innocent appearance hoodwinked me.
No magazine is safe within your claws.
Your feline mind is bent on deviltry.

How nimbly you ascend the tallest tree
in full pursuit of bits of fur and wing,
yet, failing of your hunted prey, you'll be
content to chase a dangled piece of string.
I cuddle you and call you *dearest cat*.
And sometimes, only sometimes, you are that.

*Laura J. Bobrow*

## SOMETIMES I CLEAN

When strangers come to visit me
I clean, though ordinarily
the cat and I are quite content
to live with what's expedient.

But give me notice and I jump
to give each pillowcase a thump,
to wax the wood, wash windowpanes
till not a dirty spot remains.

Each room is squeaky white-glove clean.
There's not a dust ball to be seen.
What's in the closets and the drawers
is my affair and none of yours.

Then, as the doorbell rings, I see
upon the rug, conspicuously,
a fuzzy-wuzzy tattered mouse.
The cat has spoiled my perfect house.

I thought his toys were put away.
He's brought it forth as if to say,
*Let's not pretend what we are not,*
and left it in his favorite spot.

*Laura J. Bobrow*

## DEAR CAT

Within my sacred writing spot
I am queen, and you are not.
There is one chair, on which I sit.
Your august bottom would not fit.

Within my sacred writing site
pure inspiration fills the night.
Your mewing can't disrupt the Zen
within my sacred writing den.

*Laura J. Bobrow*

## TO THE CAT WHO IS LYING ON
## MY MANUSCRIPT

If you were I, and I were you,
that is to say, a cat, or
if you were tiny as a flea
it wouldn't be a factor.
But here you are, impeding my
magnificent new opus.
You purr, you stretch. You're making it
impossible to focus.

And now you've torn it up, not just by
silly accident. You
have got that look upon your face. I think
you really meant to.
As for the work, I was, myself, somewhat
a doubting Thomas.
You're such a naughty cat!
But as a critic you show promise.

*Laura J. Bobrow*

## TO HIS PERSON

When there's wind in the oak trees
you might hear my voice.
I left you too soon
but I hadn't a choice.

When the raindrops fall lightly,
pronouncing my name,
you'll know I am near,
though it won't be the same.

Be sure to pet Bobby,
and tell Rose, *Meow*.
If mice raid the pantry
I can't help them now.

If I could, I'd be with you.
But here I am. Gone.
You're left there without me.
You must carry on.

So plump up the pillows
and turn off the light.
Be brave, human person.
I kiss you good night.

*Sarah Das Gupta*

## PRINCESS PIAYALI

Princess Piayali, Burmese cat, chocolate fur deliciously
    smooth,
feline prima donna in a household of bumbling canines.
Reigning over the sitting room, demanding unquestioning
    allegiance,
she accepts no rival, especially that upstart, brash television;
tail twitching, she walks the mantelpiece tightrope,
sending the "Gifts from Brighton" knick-knacks tumbling
    down.
At night, she tops the pyramid of sleeping canines;
Queen of the Nile, she expects humble obeisance
from the snoring horde beneath!
She joins in the start of doggy walks,
skipping and prancing down the stony lane,
only to hide in a hedge to ambush the returning hounds!
Her intelligence is centuries ahead
of her canine rivals and human admirers.
If by chance shut in, no mess to be cleared,
she delicately uses the bathroom plug hole.
Other cats—tabbies, ginger, black—have come and gone,
but none that we so desolately mourn!

*Shelley Minden*

## TELL THE BEES

> *In keeping with a centuries-old tradition, some*
> *European beekeepers draw on rituals to inform*
> *their hives of deaths and other important events*
> *in the household.*

Please someone tell the bees
Put black cloth on their hives
Place funeral bread nearby
My Tabby died

Please someone tell the bees
We'd crouch with flinging string
The floor became a field
of butterflies

Please someone tell the bees
She blanketed my knees
The reading chair turned raft
on fairy seas

Please someone tell the bees
Asleep, side to small side
we rode the moon to climb
the startled sky

Please someone tell the bees
Since Tabby died
the magic's flown
my home's just wood and stone

*Elise Chadwick*

## HOW TO GET ADOPTED

Early on a Saturday morning
before the bustle of the day,
strike a pose. Meow a friendly
yowl. When she cracks the door
to investigate, look your fluffiest
and just a tiny bit forlorn. Cross any
of your 18 toes. Make hypnotic
eye contact and hope she welcomes
you in. Pause to wipe your paws,
a well-mannered ruse you use
to stake your claim. If she offers
you a saucer of milk, never mind
your lactose intolerance. Impress her
with your lapping elegance. She will
learn with time. Keep your shedding
to a minimum.

So she puts you out? Don't despair.
Return, repeat, and return again.
You have won her over when she
takes you for a drive to a place
of white coats. Remember, the pain
and humiliation will be a faint memory
when you lounge in a ray of sunlight,
nestle on a scruffy afghan, eat
2 squares a day and entertain
your human by romping
for catnip in a feather teaser
cast out then reeled in
on a fishing line.

*Michael Spence*

## STEPCAT

*Let's go to Maple Valley—the vet*
*Says there's a place where we can get*

*An orange tabby*, my wife said.
*I've wanted one since I was a kid.*

The drive took us to a huge house
Where a couple kept a huddled mass

Of kittens. *They've all been abandoned*
*In the woods behind our place*, explained

The owner; *some people just believe*
*They'll become wild again and survive.*

The first one brave enough, despite
Our presence, to come and take a bite

From a food bowl was the tabby. *He'll let*
*You pet him only when he eats.*

My wife and I took turns stroking him;
He paid no heed. But on the way home,

He howled in his cage. We named him Blake
After "The Tyger." We tried not to make

Any sudden move or loud noise
Around him. Scared of most of the toys

We tossed his way, he'd run and hide.
But he'd jump on the couch, sit beside

My wife and stretch out as if made
Of taffy. She smiled: *You're not afraid*

*Of us, are you, taffy tabby?*
Maybe he thought we could only grab

Him if we were standing. For years,
He'd run ahead as we climbed the stairs,

Not letting us get near. Then one day,
He surprised me by stopping halfway

Up, tilting his head toward me. I said
As I rubbed it, *Blake, I'm really glad—*

*Although I hear that green and blue
Are rarer—your eyes are orange as you.*

I felt for the first time the ridge
In his skull beneath the fur. He edged

Up a step, stopped for a pet,
Then it was up-stop-pet-repeat.

Reaching the top, I felt him brush
My hand as he headed to the food dish.

Michael Spence

## OPENING A DOOR

Brought up with dogs, I figured cats
Were not real pets. The pair a friend owned
Either ignored him or ran around
Like Tasmanian devils. If one sat

On my lap, a sudden sound would inject
Its claws into my leg. When the wife
Said *Let's get two*, I felt the grief
They'd bring. Cats would never act

As keen as a dog—you can't chase
Them in the back yard, ruffle their fur.
I said the cats would have to be *her*
Responsibility: I'd pass.

When she drove off, she took her mom
Who had to fight to keep the lid
On the box holding them. They tried
To escape when put in the back room,

But my wife jumped out and closed the door.
*If you want to see the kittens, make sure
They stay shut in.* Never fear,
I shook my head; I won't go in there.

She frowned but said nothing. Next day
She left for work. All was quiet
Behind the door. Maybe I ought
To take a peek? Ducking through,

I shut it quick and glanced around.
The top of her writing desk, the floor,
Under the ergonomic chair,
Everywhere—I couldn't find

A trace. Had I let them escape?
My wife would hate me. And why not?
I pulled out the chair to sit
And think about what to do. And stopped:

On the cushion lay two lumps of fur,
Blinking. Slowly, I reached to stroke
A forehead. Both pulled back,
Jumping down to hide in the corner.

*Michael Spence*

## IN WINTER: MOVE & COUNTERMOVE

The wedge of light the sun, just risen, sends
Through the window lays its length along the rug.
The smaller black-and-white cat, first to find
This patch, sits down in its glow, stretching legs
As though floating on a little raft of heat.
The orange tabby watches her a while
Then comes over and licks her head and throat
Until she moves: she jumps up on the sill
That he's too big to fit on. The patch belongs
To him—he sprawls in its gleam, stripes turned bright
As deep copper. She moves once more, casting
Him in darkness as she blocks the light.

Henriëtte Ronner-Knip, *St. Nicholas series*

*Diane Stone*

## TO NAME A CAT

*The Naming of Cats is a difficult matter,*
*It isn't just one of your holiday games;*
from "The Naming of Cats"
*Old Possum's Book of Practical Cats*
T. S. Eliot

*Fluffy* isn't the right name for her;
she's really not that fluffy, except for her tail.
Nor is she slender enough to be called *Slim*
nor plump enough to be called *Chubby*.
Her fur is orange-ish, so maybe *Pumpkin* will do
or even *Ginger* or *Amber*.
She eats only beef pâté, never chicken or fish.
Should I name her *Picky* or *Princess*?

I thought about *Noisy* because she yowls,
but that's so obvious, and today she's silent
as a cat ghost, sleeping most of the day.

Okay, maybe *Pumpkin*, but since her fur
reminds me of gusty autumn weather,
how about *Sunbeam* or *Zephyr*?
Actually, *Fluffy* might be okay or *Pumpkin*.
But definitely not *Chubby* or *Princess*.
*Kitty* would do in a pinch. Or even *Cat*.

*Daniel Thomas Moran*

## HITCHENS THE CAT

Sometimes, I think
he thinks
I am a bed.

Sometimes, I think
he thinks
I am a bathtub.

Sometimes, I think
he thinks
I am a masseuse.

Sometimes, I think
he thinks
I am a food truck.

Sometimes, I think
he thinks
I am a brush.

Sometimes, I think
he thinks
I am a chew toy.

Sometimes, I think
he thinks
I am a bird.

Sometimes, I think
he thinks
I am a magician.

Sometimes, I think
he thinks
I am his mother.

Sometimes, I think
he thinks
I am a faucet.

Sometimes, I think
he thinks
I am another cat.

*Larry Needham*

## THE CAT'S WHISKERS

Hear sung the Song of Singh—Thomas Singh—the
    sing-song ditty
of a sleeping tom, drowsing in the hearth's warm glow,
    secure
from glowering firedogs, combusting logs—*ahhh, safe*:
    how he purred
his deep content, dreaming of sacral fires and vestal
    kitties—

worthy of a snooze or catnap, no? when—more's the pity—
a dormant log caught fire, blazed into a brand, and burst,
a firework shower of sparks singeing paws, lids, nose, but
    worse,
scorching the brave whiskers of our feline Walter Mitty

who, dismayed and sickened, fled the household and the city
he'd called home and struck out for the wilds, some natural
    retreat
where he might hide his shame and heal burnt nose, ears,
    padded feet.
But his whiskers, would they sprout again, just an itty-bitty?

For the sight reflected in a pool wasn't very pretty.
No lip lace upon his face, weary from exposure,
caught up in catastrophe, Thomas lost composure
(to sacrifice a lady's lap was a crying pity).

Whiskerless, Thomas wandered in the wilderness *à midi*,
then sat beneath a weeping tree (sing willow, willow, willow)
and wept his cat's eyes dry—he was a sorry, sallow fellow—
until, emptied like a pitcher, Tom turned sudden giddy

at the sight of catkins drooping pale in sad committee,
listless, limp—the image of his detumescent spirit—
(for if Nature sings a Psalm of Life, Thomas couldn't hear it),
and he wryly laughed until he ached in unabashed self-pity.

Tom roused himself, following a stream, crystalline and
    pretty,
for where there's a willow, there's a waterway, which he
    traced
to a boggy, soggy wetland marsh, a soppy, spongy place
alive with reeds and cattails. How that vision turned him
    giddy!

He flashed and dashed among the stalks, a resurrected kitty,
chasing cattails that waved before his eyes—until he
    pounced
to bow them with retracted claws or press them ounce by
    ounce
down to the muddy bottom—the earthy nitty-gritty.

Bulrushes at his feet and punks that itched a little bitty
when drawn beneath his nose (he looked a bit like Groucho),
the dank, rank smell of cheap cheroots made Tom Cat feel
    macho.
An ersatz stache above his lip? Why, he was sitting pretty!

All day he'd catch, then set the cattails free, from a well of
    pity,
to hunt again, tufts of fluff on his face—and does so to this
    day.
So if from weedy reeds you hear a growl or see a cat at play,
know it's Tom—Thomas Singh—sung hero of this
    sing-song ditty.

*John Grey*

## YOUR CATS

In your house, many cats roam free.
And your ceramic felines are
in a state of just about to.
Tabby mobiles tinkle in the wind.
Even your wallpaper is on the lookout
for an unwitting mouse to creep out of a hole.
Your Persians shed. Your Siamese purr.
When the lights go down, their eyes take over.
Every room is a night sky twinkling with green stars.

Alarie Tennille

*When the pupil is ready, the teacher will come.*
Chinese proverb

Before showing us any moves,
our t'ai chi instructor lectures
for forty-five minutes. *Good chi enter*
*head. Bad chi leave through feet.*

I grow stiff on philosophy, but perk
up with his warning that cats steal
our chi. It's especially dangerous
when they sleep on our pillows—

no wonder I'm too tired to concentrate.
Cats are hotter than humans,
and apparently I am the power outlet
for three purring radiators, twelve feet

to clean of negative energy as they stomp
around my lap. I'd welcome a sunny
windowsill about now. Picture my three
cats awaiting my return. I'm ready

to copy their Zen state. Finally!
We are invited to stand, raise our arms
overhead, and sink our chi. I look around
at clumsy humans. No one stretches

with feline elegance. No one can leap
six times his height. I'm dropping
this class and going home to study
the real masters.

*Rick Clark*

## LITTLE BEAR HAIKU

I play violin
out the window—coaxing
the cat back home


taking a cat
for a friend—be prepared
for the silent treatment


sitting on the deck—
my head turns with the cat's
at spring's first frog-croak


how long it hovers—
the dragonfly studying
our sleeping cat

the old cat turns round
four times before curling up
into a ball


the cat in his grave:
may that guy finally play
his fiddle in tune!


hardened atheist—
hearing his cat cry out
from beneath his cairn


catches himself
about to pet the cairn—
his old cat's grave

*Rick Clark*

## CAT TAO

How does our cat know
where next to lick?
Why the nonexistent balls
just after the lifted thigh?

Why flop down
against the wall
and not on a pillow today?
Why not on my lap?

A crow's caw in the distance
turns an ear
so his tongue hesitates,
a moment's recognition,

then he goes on licking,
knowing the one true way.

*Rick Clark*

## CAT LOVE

Our cat can't hide his love.
He plays hard to get, turns away.
Miffed, he stalks off peeved,
flicks his tail, biting fleas
he no longer has.

Our cat can't hide his love.
In the end he pads up on my chest
where I lie on my back
dead with fatigue and half asleep,
and demands, with full abandonment
to looking the fool,
all the love in my sleepy state
I can muster.

He drools on my neck,
looks me, finally, straight in the eye,
his whole shimmering feline face
beginning to smile.

Our cat can't hide his love.
He purrs louder and louder,
the bed begins to tremble
and, beginning to grin,
I wonder what was ever
the matter with this world.

*Jack Granath*

## THE TAO OF ATTICUS

My old cat's sleep is like the pre-Creation,
His stretch is like dawn rising from its den,
His roll is like a planet's grand rotation,
And then he winks and goes to sleep again.
Some darkness made me name him Atticus,
While better names lay scattered all around:
Omar, Lao Tzu, Sardanapalus.
So on a lonely day he got miscrowned.
I envy him, full-bellied little bum,
But know I can't live my short life like that.
Art is unyielding. These lines do not come
As easily as dreams do to a cat.

I can't approve his life, but I *would* love it,
And that's the fine, feline seduction of it.

*Carolyn Adams*

## WHAT COMFORT

I still have the grace of my recline.
If you ask me what I'm thinking,
I'll tell you, "My decline,"
because that's simpler.
I know the meaning of
the word "terminal,"
but its reminder doesn't consume
that much of my day, my nights,
my time left with you.
I know you need my warmth
in the days that remain.
The various greens of my
eyes linger on the things
you do each hour. I watch
as you prepare your meals
and clean your belongings
in this sunny room.
I listen
to the calls of birds outside
and the small sounds of
mammals I might prey upon.
I know they're out of my reach
for now, maybe for always.
I lean on you,
drape your lap, and give you
what comfort I can.

*Sheila Bender*

## CAT IN MY LAP

1.
A cat must drink a lot of water to replace
the water he uses to lick himself clean.

A mother who has lost her son must drink
a lot of water to fill the ocean of her grief.


2.
My dreams have a dripping faucet,
the cat lapping and lapping what he can.

I return to sleep hoping for a river
and a bowl to fill.


3.
After we moved houses, I sat
under trumpet vines drinking espresso
among businesspeople at white tables,
pollen dusting their sandwiches.

In our new apartment, the cat slept,
tired from so much shedding.

4.

Mornings, my cat presses his paw gently on the space
between my brows. I wake believing he wants
me to know that he is hungry, until I learn
it is the Ajna Chakra he touches and me who hungers
to see beyond the physical.


5.

I sit this night at my desk breathless
at the brightness of the moon outside my window.

The cat jumps to the sill, her tail merely
an eyelash caught in the moonshine.

*Barbara Johnstone*

## Entranced worshiper

on the windowsill, paws uplifted
to the sun god, Ra. Chaser of shadow
and light. Stealth computer writer with
tufted-quiet toes. Determined book
interrupter, lap rug, head warmer and
oh, luxury! auburn black stole.
Contortionist in the cat tree, shaker
in the empty tub, fuzzy towel on the linen shelf.
Squatter on any square item. Mantle
leaper, 2:00 a.m. off-the-table plop.
Ragdoll. Narrator in hoarse whispers.
Dreamer—as superman spread in flight.
Then—slowly—after sixteen years—
leaper and climber no more
while I—failed commander of
*Off the table, Come here, Don't*
*jump your little sis*—am nurse reader
of his shadow and light. I tender salmon
and pharmaceuticals until,
written in his amber eyes—*Do it, goodbye.*

*Judith Shapiro*

## FELINE LOVE

On our way home from the funeral
we stopped for gas at a highway exit.
It was dark and raining.

She was at the dumpster, hanging with feral cats.
She screamed for us to pick her up,
grey striped tail covered in mud.

*Don't put that cat in my car,* you said.
*But we'll name her Claire Estelle*, we said,
*after your mother*.

Fifteen years later
the last one standing from our little tribe of found misfits
she is failing.

I bury my face in her warm fur
marveling at her perfection
as I will her to live forever.

*Lana Hechtman Ayers*

## THE SHOVEL

The hole outside the sunroom
needed to be dug deep but
stone by stone, dirt refused the shovel.
Gravel gave way to cave-ins.
As if Earth were declining
the offering to be placed within.
Not a rosebush, not a maple tree,
not a half dozen daffodil bulbs,
but one domestic cat,
body stiff with rigor mortis,
fur matted to homogeneous gray,
one swollen eye gone to cloud.

A cat in life called Federico Rodolpho.
A romantic name,
heavy mantle for a light cat,
sharp cheekbones,
pointy antenna ears,
who loved riding on shoulders like a parrot,
fetching toys like a retriever,
who had been with us a mere two years
before the specialist's failed intervention
into a mysterious disease.
Two short years of feline bliss,
a cat to be missed a lifetime afterward.

In the end, the shovel triumphed
as it always does,
death's earthbound accomplice.

*Elizabeth Kerlikowske*

## ELEGY FOR ASH

Her grave is her home as of yesterday
dug the day before, before she died.
My death coach said it had to be that way.

Our cat was calm and sleek and ashy gray,
good at every feline trick she tried
but her grave is her home as of yesterday.

Bigger than the rest, she softly played
and enjoyed nothing more than a good hide.
My death coach said it had to be that way.

The coach said to let the cat decide the day,
the place, the time, the way she wants to die
to her grave, her home since yesterday.

Some advice can be difficult to obey
but we got her to the other side.
Her grave is her home as of yesterday;
my death coach said to cry away.

*Sharon Hashimoto*

# MAPLE CREST APARTMENTS
## —Summer, 2021

I

A column of black rises over the hill
like a tail flicking before a cat's
pounce. Wisps of white steam waver
with the wind while the caterwauling
of a siren shrieks up and down, joined
by a second and third yowl-yowl-yowl.


II

Like the bread crumbs Hansel and Gretel
scattered to follow home, the posters appear
on chain-link fences and telephone poles.
There's Jax, neutered male, striped with a kinked tail.
Brothers with white blazes and whiskers. Eight cats,
two dogs. Neighbors leave food out at dusk and dawn.


III

Ears pulled back, crouched low to the ground,
was the calico hiding at the farthest corner
under the bed? Did the smoke cloud the blue eyes
of the harlequin, sullying the white fur? Or did
the black cat dodge under tables and hurdle chairs,
racing for the cooler air, the open door?

IV

A week or ten days later—rain
patters against posterboard. Tape sags.
Photos streak and smear, ink draining down.

*Sharon Hashimoto*

## OSCAR PREDICTS

Close to the floor, but with the brush
of a tail held high, the cat lightly pads
down the linoleum hall. Oscar weaves

through the rooms—many holding a chair,
a bureau, a twin bed, sometimes a quilt
tucked high around the shoulders

of an elder. He dodges the outstretched
hands of family to reach the one lost
in fading fragments of memory

of the sun against eyelids, the notes
of a sparrow rising in song. He leaps
to a pillow, beside the woman's gray hair

spread like a fan, to sniff her face and skin,
to settle his fur against her neck. *Go home,*
a nurse tells the family, *you need to rest.*

The woman's body stills. The hills her lungs
have climbed level out. She's not alone.
For her last few hours, Oscar is there.

_Sharon Hashimoto_

## BUS STOP AT HANAPEPE

Everyone seated on the bench has black
sweat-shined hair. A woman in a faded dress
speaks to the boy over the open shoebox
sandwiched between them. They mount the steps

to the bus, the boy hugging the box. Inside, on a piece
of white toweling, a black kitten lies on its side,
nostrils flared, whistling each breath.
The driver shivers at the token's clatter.

She doesn't know if she croons, _shh shh_
to the boy, the cat, or to the bus
bumping and hitching to another stop.
Hair strands escape their knot; the heat
from her hand bakes the boy's fingers. There's a vet
in the next small city. She thinks, _he's three years old._
She watches as his eyes
keep following the folds in the towel.

The boy studies the ellipse of the kitten's ear,
how one white whisker echoes the line of the jaw.
He wants to tell his mother, _Tama's eyes are open!_
His arm hairs stand up like fur.

*Katherine Meizel*

## THE STRAY

A cobweb fog clung to the night we met
and caught your cry of fury in mid-air.
Alone, you tiger-paced the office steps;
the footlights backed your infant silhouette.

And once at home, at once you staked your claim,
all under-spaces turned to hygge nests,
the table and piano to grand veldts
for you to stalk your spectral, unseen game.

Now no thing's safe and sounds slip past my door
from your tornado midnights, while I sleep.
Your secret wars with cushions are laid bare
when sunbeams light the wreckage on the floor.

Still, each time fever grips you I'd forgive
the greatest cat transgression, if you'd live.

## David Sheskin

# AUTOPSY OF OUR CAT

Her doctor tells us
He is of the opinion
She had traveled far and wide
That once upon a time
She had wandered into a rain forest
And swallowed a fluorescent butterfly
Had penetrated a knotty crevice
And aroused the wrath of a slimy serpent
Ascended a towering tree
And purloined the egg of a cuckoo bird
Had dived into the waters of the Caspian
And feasted on the roe of wild sturgeon
Had plumbed a forgotten catacomb
And walked among the withering skeletons of our
ancestors
Who knew that beneath
Those mysterious eyes
Lingered secrets
Of a double life
While all the while we thought
She was on our bed
Nestled within the cocoon of
A peaceful slumber

*Kelli Russell Agodon*

## TODAY I QUESTIONED LOVE,

asked her why she was always asleep
in my life, yet still I have scratch marks
down my back, on my arms. Love
doesn't say much, instead, she knocks
a spoon off the coffee table as if she's bored
with all I ask. Love goes into the kitchen
to get something to eat, she never asks
if I'm hungry too, and I say, *Love
I am ravenous*. Love ignores me. Love
doesn't even care whether I am here
or not. I tell Love how she never
greets me at the door, and when I call
for her, Love never answers. And yet,
here we are, living together, her now asleep
on the couch and me trying not to
get in her way, but I guess this really is
what love is, two creatures sharing space,
which is what I do with this small black
cat named Love I brought into my home.

# Kelli Russell Agodon

## SURREALIST WOMEN GROW(L)ING FROM LEMON TREES

*There are many tigers in one lemon.*
Amanda Berenguer from "el limón"
translated by Gayle Brandeis

And when I bite, it bites back.
A tangle of rivers where tigers drink
and I dive in to the pack.

We have no keeper, we are tigers, women
who sip nectar from the beak
        of a hummingbird

then tame lions with the tip of our pen.
        We hold the zest that moves us
while others keep the bitter,

taste only the sour of what jungles
have to offer. Sometimes, the world
growls and we bite back.

Sometimes we are a pack, we resist and rest,
other times the world reveals its sweetness
the thing that we devour.

*Rainer Maria Rilke*

## DER PANTHER

*Im Jardin des Plantes, Paris*

Sein Blick ist vom Vorübergehn der Stäbe
so müd geworden, daß er nichts mehr hält.
Ihm ist, als ob es tausend Stäbe gäbe
und hinter tausend Stäben keine Welt.

Der weiche Gang geschmeidig starker Schritte,
der sich im allerkleinsten Kreise dreht,
ist wie ein Tanz von Kraft um eine Mitte,
in der betäubt ein großer Wille steht.

Nur manchmal schiebt der Vorhang der Pupille
sich lautlos auf —. Dann geht ein Bild hinein,
geht durch der Glieder angespannte Stille —
und hört im Herzen auf zu sein.

Susan McLean

## THE PANTHER

by Rainer Maria Rilke, translated by Susan McLean

*In the Botanical Garden, Paris*

From passing by the endless bars, his gaze
has wearied till there's nothing it can hold.
It seems to him there are a thousand bars,
and out beyond the thousand bars, no world.

The soft tread of his powerful, lithe stride
that turns in circles of the smallest size
is like a dance of strength around a void
in which a mighty will stands paralyzed.

Only at times the pupils' curtains rise
soundlessly—. An image enters them,
passes in silent tension through each limb—
then lodges in his heart and dies.

Rainer Maria Rilke

## SCHWARZE KATZE

Ein Gespenst ist noch wie eine Stelle,
dran dein Blick mit einem Klange stößt;
aber da, an diesem schwarzen Felle
wird dein stärkstes Schauen aufgelöst:

wie ein Tobender, wenn er in vollster
Raserei ins Schwarze stampft,
jählings am benehmenden Gepolster
einer Zelle aufhört und verdampft.

Alle Blicke, die sie jemals trafen,
scheint sie also an sich zu verhehlen,
um darüber drohend und verdrossen
zuzuschauern und damit zu schlafen.
Doch auf einmal kehrt sie, wie geweckt,
ihr Gesicht und mitten in das deine:
und da triffst du deinen Blick im geelen
Amber ihrer runden Augensteine
unerwartet wieder: eingeschlossen
wie ein ausgestorbenes Insekt.

*Susan McLean*

# BLACK CAT

by Rainer Maria Rilke, translated by Susan McLean

Even a ghost is like a place your stare
bumps into with a sound that resonates,
but here, against this inky pelt of fur,
your strongest gazes will disintegrate,

just as a raving madman when, brimful
of rage, he stomps into the night,
in the restraining padding of a cell
abruptly calls it quits and peters out.

All of the glances that have ever hit her
she seems to carry on her under wraps,
so that, morose and menacing, she later
may watch and brood upon them as she sleeps.
As if awakened, all at once she turns
her countenance directly toward your own,
and unexpectedly you meet again
your own gaze there within the yellow stones
of her round amber eyes, in which you're locked
as though you are an insect long extinct.

*Charles Baudelaire*

## LE CHAT

Viens, mon beau chat, sur mon coeur amoureux;
Retiens les griffes de ta patte,
Et laisse-moi plonger dans tes beaux yeux,
Mêlés de métal et d'agate.

Lorsque mes doigts caressent à loisir
Ta tête et ton dos élastique,
Et que ma main s'enivre du plaisir
De palper ton corps électrique,

Je vois ma femme en esprit. Son regard,
Comme le tien, aimable bête
Profond et froid, coupe et fend comme un dard,

Et, des pieds jusques à la tête,
Un air subtil, un dangereux parfum
Nagent autour de son corps brun.

*Susan McLean*

## THE CAT

by Charles Baudelaire, translated by Susan McLean

My lovely cat, come, sheathe your claws
and on my loving heart lie prone,
letting me plumb your gorgeous eyes,
where metal's sheen meets agate's stone.

For as my fingers leisurely
caress your head and supple back,
sensing your body's energy
with each intoxicated stroke,

I see my mistress in my heart.
Like yours, my charming beast, her gaze,
profound and cold, cuts like a dart,

while from her, head to foot, there strays
a faint perfume, a subtle hint
of her dark body's dangerous scent.

Félix Vallotton, *La Paresse*

*Kris Michelle Diesness*

## FELINE PARALYSIS

To be covered in cats—
a peculiar treat—
to be kneaded and treaded by soft, tiny feet.
The weight of their warmth lightly pulsing with purrs,
burrowed in blankets as soft as their furs.
Unwilling to move from this most-cozy spot,
I succumb to my captors, more often than not.

*Kris Michelle Diesness*

## SNOW LEOPARD

The soft crunch of stealthy paws on crisp, frosted peaks
folds into the quiet cold of mountain clouds.
Snow Leopard,
hidden in white mists
while night's shroud of stars
calls sleep to deep caves
beckoning Her to rest.
Through cycles and seasons,
in waking and in dreams,
solitude speaks
from the edge of instinct,
guiding Her silent quest to conquer.

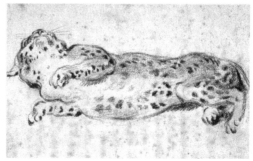

Jean-Antoine Watteau, *Jéune leopard s'étirant*

*Margaret Chula*

**TANKA**

in Sri Lanka
climbing the rocky trail
to World's End
we chant to scare off
the chuffing leopard

## Margaret Chula

## TOMCAT

I never thought you'd come back into my life,
but there you were curled up on my front porch.
A stray, belonging to no one. It was you, Tom.
I could tell from your first meow. It sounded
like my name. You recognized me, too.
Tracked me down after all these years.
Your sense of smell was always good—
patchouli, after-tennis sweat, gumdrops.
You could always smell me coming.

After fifty years, you still have a full head of hair.
Your green eyes flash as I pick you up, gently,
like a bottle of milk left on the doorstep.
You snuggle against my breasts, pink negligee
soothing you as we lounge on the velvet settee.
Your head in my lap, I caress you like yesterday.
Whisper Grateful Dead lyrics into your ear.

Your legs twitch, toes curl. Yes, I remember
how my caresses made you happy—
your long sighs and sweet nothings.
And later, how your sharp nails
came out when it was over.

Benjamin S. Grossberg

## THE NEXT WORLD

Three years gone, the dog will greet me there.
She'll waggle up to my arms at the pearly gate.
A spitz with wet glass eyes and fine white hair,
she was nearly an angel in her earthly state—
with just as much free will as angels have,
her nature to please mine, to show how grace
can elevate obedience into love
and turn a wolf's into an angel's face.

But if things go south, at least there'll be my cat—
soot fur with eyes that flash like yellow tin.
She'll help the devils rend my flesh, a blur
of arch and hiss, of claw, ears back and flat.
She shows the gross indifference of sin
then implicates me with a little purr.

*Stuart Stromin*

## CATS BY DOGS

They are cunning little creatures
And impossible to catch.
Among their deadly features
Is how precisely they can scratch.

They can mimic the human voice—
An advantage in the house—
And make the humans rejoice
When they bring in a dead mouse.

Cats do not know how to bark
And are limited in hearing,
But they see right through the dark
And are skilled at disappearing.

They can jump as high as tables
And climb up chairs and drapes,
With nine lives in the fables
Because of their close escapes.

*Beware of Dog* is the old sign,
*Beware of Cat*, none warns,
But that furry friendly feline
Is a cuddle full of thorns.

*Sheryl Clough*

## SAM AND SNOWPAWS

In the vee of our old acacia tree
perched our calico cat Snowpaws,
waiting with barely restrained glee

for the moment she'd swipe her claws
across Sam our Samoyed's snout.
It must be one of Nature's laws:

dogs must chase and cats must rout
them, must stifle every frenzied chase
so cats may leisurely go about

their lazy days with measured grace.
Poor Sam could never win a round;
always ended with cat-scratched face.

You never saw a more dejected hound.
Sam whimpered under that acacia tree
and Snowpaws gloated at the sound.

*Betty Benson*

## SAY YOU LOVE HER

Say you love her, and she killed your cat. Say
she drove your car, put a dent in your new
Subaru; spilled on your shirt, cabernet,
an oaky cassis, then what would you do?

You had a cat once, beautiful, but bad;
fierce, yellow eyes glittered with feral light.
She liked to bite you, run across your head
as you tried, in vain, to sleep through the night.

More than once you said you wanted to kill
that cat, shake all the badness out of her,
but you were no match for her feline will.
How could you know what your heart would endure

at end—what more is love than to forgive?
When her eyes bid, *say you love me*, then you did.

*Judith Skillman*

## ALL SWEETNESS

Does my cat—*le chat, el gato, kot*—
have as many names as space and time?
To take communion I kneel at his paws.
To soothe abandonment I pet him,
listen to the rumble of his purr.
All lamb is my lion, a tortoiseshell
with large head, long tail, and regal ears.
When the house quiets he returns. Well

he knows children. Gentle is royalty,
a coat thicker than new-fallen snow.
Silky fur threads my fingers, undoes ennui.
The mole he brings: broad-chested, just so.
He lays it beneath a cherry chair.
For hours I prefer to leave it there.

§

For hours I prefer to leave it here,
this rodent brought in by a cat honed
to sense. If even a small part comes near
his sight—the Maine Coon's heavily boned.
Built for barn work, thick-legged, broad
in the chest. Instinctual hunter.
Digging into labyrinthine sod
and digging faster he'll bring her

to the surface. A pounce, a puncture
and it's over. How can I adore
a feline who kills not out of hunger?
It's all play to him. I stood here

when another cat, former beloved,
ate a house mouse. Company stayed, unfazed.

§

Ah, the house mouse. Company stayed, unfazed
by scenes of barbarism. An era
when, our children young, house mouse lived
in a sack of flour. We knew *a la*
the sound of paper tearing, nights.
My daughter found it in a vase,
threw it outside, midwinter. What a sight.
Large, gray, long-tailed. Our rampant distaste

for this innocent largely outstripped
its humble desire to remain alive.
To return to the Maine Coon. Gripped
and crippled, *bury me*, I say, give
him not lip service but instruction.
I cannot live without this cat as kin.

§

I can't live without a cat as kin.
His presence the Holy Magi star
around which elder hours seem to turn.
Lifespan—seven to thirteen years.
Loyal, he sleeps next to dirty shoes
in the hallway, wakes to eat, watch birds,
snooze in summer sun. I wonder whose
more human, him or me? His days conclude

with gratitude. Each moment is just that.
Nothing's wanting to be done. A puzzle:
with one paw one side of his face, washed. What

follows? A pinkish toe pulled to muzzle.
I've learned that to a cat, blink means smile.
We look and *blink-blink-blink* awhile.

§

We look and *blink-blink-blink* awhile.
For metaphysics, draw a cat. Bonnard's.
Holes for eyes, tail striped, held up until
what matters doesn't anymore. Hard
to laugh and worry in the same instant.
Animal grows closer than a lover.
I talk to this genie as if he could grant
three wishes. What would they be? Lure

my body away from doing. Let one
be content with nothing. Allow enough
to be enough. Silky fur, bars of sun
and tiger stripes. When afraid, up he puffs.
Afraid, I grow small, seek solace in what
is. My cat. *El gato, kot, le chat.*

*Judith Skillman*

## HOMAGE & LAMENT

Let in the door my other lives,
the ones that died, my loves
for whom I grieved so hard
it seems absurd
they were feline.
Worse than the death of any human—
a friend of mine agreed.
She'd suffered more from the loss
of her childhood pet, a cat,
than when a close relative passed.
The pattern's clear—
we are no more owners
of our cats than staff.
We do whatever the eff
they want us to
without a thought, though
it may mean staying home
instead of going out.
Could it be their company
pleases us despite the
arse-licking in our presence,
the raised tail—most
of all the disregard,
the way their green or hard
yellow eyes see so well?
Always the same lull
after this one,
before the next comes along
wearing fur coat & pajamas.
Not caring whether any of us
remain on the bus,

looking into the distance,
assuming the stance
a hunter takes
when stalking snakes,
rodents, or, most like winter wind,
come to remind
the inferior species (human)
of its imperfection.

*Griffith Williams*

## PHOEBE'S PROOF

So, our premise begins "If this, then that."
Now, "that" is a home and "this" is a cat.
Then there by the door, where I've hung my hat,
True logic presumes…. Well, look at the mat:
A tuft of fur shows where a feline sat.
        And the feline proves your house is a home
        And that in turn proves the truth of this poem.

## Ina Roy-Faderman

Bellicose, the cat

tips the stacked boxes,
Amazon's millions
nothing to his paws.

Henriëtte Ronner-Knip, *Katjesspel*

*Cathy Bryant*

## THE CAT SAT...

The cat sat on the raffia mat
The cat sat on the table.
The cat sat almost anywhere
that a canny cat is able.

The cat napped on the clean dry clothes
The cat napped on his head.
The cat napped on the just-bloomed rose
but not on his cat bed.

*Ace Boggess*

## LAST MEOW

Imagine a cat
made of chocolate.

As it licks itself clean,
it slowly disappears.

Henriëtte Ronner-Knip, *Naschkätzchen*

_Jayne Marek_

## HEY LITTLE DIDDLE

The cat will fiddle
a ball down the hall
and a twist of paper
flips head over

Hey little little
how wet with spittle
how loved this mouse toy
with ears so ragged

Hey in the middle
of the open cupboard
of a heap of laundry
of the kitchen floor

O that skitter skitter
of whatever whatever
o that thump thump
of something against wood

Diddle till you trip us
fiddle till you stop us
from whatever we do
until we tend to you

*Tom Barlow*

## THREE HAIKU

Cat butts the front door;
I open it—too cold outside.
She heads for the back door.


Vacuum sweepers growl
the predator roams the den
cats on high alert


Cat in the window
watches birds, dreams of murder
sweet little snookums

*Art Gomez*

## BUT I NEED MY MEOW TIME

You see, it's like this
The novelty of 24/7
has worn thin

"Kitty - Kitty"
throughout the day
was cool, until I realized
it was not about me
(as it should be)
it was about you
We both know
That-Cat-Won't-Mouse


*Stop        changing*
*    the subject    with*
*              that      damn      laser*
*    light*


Back to business:
- Fill my bowls
- Clean my box
- Go outside and play…. Please

That should tell you something about my desperation
I'm a cat and I'm saying, "Please"

*Linda Jenkinson*

## FALSE ALARM

The intruder broke security
In the dead of night.
The honking cacophony
Alerted geese in southern flight
Who looked below with watchful eye,
But seeing no brethren in distress,
Added to the melody with raucous noisiness.
We woke and peered through window shades,
Leery of seeing the aftermath
And there, on the top of our honking car,
Sat our very own cat taking his bath.

*JC Reilly*

## JENNY'S MORNING RITUAL

I'm dead asleep, and little feet
begin their samba on my chest:
*Get up, get up, it's time to eat!*

5 o'clock is no time to greet
the day. I try longer to rest—
not dead asleep *now* but little feet

will not stop their steady beat.
I push the cat aside; she's a pest.
*Get up, get up, it's time to eat!*

Over my head I pull the sheets
and hunker down in my bed's nest.
I'm asleep again till little feet

begin to run across me, browbeat
me until I give in, get dressed.
*Get up, get up, it's time to eat!*

She flies to the door—how so fleet?—
Onto the kitchen like a quest.
Oh Jenny! I curse your little feet
each day it's time for you to eat.

*James B. Nicola*

## WAKING UP TO CAT

Her mighty force patrols her twilit realm.
When I, audacious Gulliver, dare to rise
she deploys all twenty bayonets in file.
Their threat against my flesh restores the calm,
then she reassumes her throne, my chest. The wise
face, the unyielding Mona Lisa smile,
sage whiskers, and the almond emerald eyes
impose such pleasant peace, though. And what harm
does she inflict, what tribute does she gain,
in shocking me to rouse now out of bed,
with nary an adjustment to the counterpane—
for after all, the monarch must be fed—
only to keep me in place, her royal purrs
reminding me these lands are really hers?

_James B. Nicola_

## NEPHEW AND CAT

The first time that he held his cat
was the minute that he met the cat.
In a flash he knew, and that was that
and he took the cat home.

The first time he was held by his cat
was not so very long after that:
He came home burning under his hat.
It didn't have a thing to do with the cat,
but the cat knew. How? Well. After that
they called each other _home_.

The last time that he held his cat
was the last time he was held by his cat.
He kissed the cat and that was that.
The cat knew, and went Home.

*Torrey Francis Malek*

## SPACE INVADER

4 AM lingers.

I pry an eye open and spy, a shape,
sifting cautiously from gapping sky.

A light glazes irised headlights, lenses,
obsidian disks hung high, overhead.

Then comes the coo of an alien
engine bellowing lowly, below them.

I'm startled.
Then bothered.

I try to retreat
deep beneath the sheets,

but this just entices
the being to pursue.

It then descends.

I can sense a shape shifting,
drifting down through ghoulish gloom.

My hand offers to amuse it, the foolish martyr,
and he dashes out into certain doom, alone.

The foreign engine hums ever harder,
my heart heaving from the wait of the unknown.

Then something shifts slightly against my palm,
calm, soft, malleable, flocculent clay.

I know then, I am given no choice:
An unconditional surrender.

I pet the tabby for
her acceptable timespan

until she is satisfied
with the expedition.

She floats back out into the dark
her mission surely deemed: [SUCCESS].

Back up to her mothership
for stringent analysis,

and so now
I may rest.

Until 5 AM lingers.

*Christopher J. Jarmick*

## ENOUGH; GOODBYE
## *OR*
## THE CAT WHO WROTE A POEM

'tis not so hard
you so-called bard
such toil and sweat
spending so much time
and some regret I see
searching for worthy rhyme
when you should be petting me
I perceive that
you shall never believe
there could ever be a poet cat.

but if you would take a closer look
at how I knead with paws
can you write that in your book?
have you such skill if for good cause?
thy language old
mine oh so bold
I know patience it would take
to listen for poetry's sake
to the sounds of my purr
the markings on my fur
'tis simple though yes?
I do confess
and so
expand your vision
make a dangerous revision
I scribble here, there
and in places where
you don't ever go

too much to say
you grumble and fail
so on my way
with majestic tail
time to leave now
this more than play
I cry, meow,
yet you won't see
my special poetry
no matter how I try
enough, enough
goodbye.

*James Rodgers*

## AILUROPHILE

As an introvert,
I appreciate cats,
their aloofness refreshing
not cloying
not needy,
willing to stand still
pretending they don't hear us
when we call their names,
only paying attention
to us,
meowing
rubbing
purring
when they feel like it
when it's their inclination,
and more nights than not
they'll climb and curl
into my wife's lap,
both felines vying
for the limited space,
leaving me free
to get up
move as I please,
but there are times
I must admit
I wish at least one
would share their warmth
their evening
with me
as even us introverts
get cold sometimes.

*James Rodgers*

## GATO SUPREME

4 cups attitude
2 cups aloofness
2 cups independence
1 cup warmth and companionship
¼ teaspoon sense of humor
4 legs
4 sets of claws
1 purr engine
1 set of whiskers
1 tail (not available on all models)

No need to measure, sift, mix, bake, or microwave. Gato Supreme is pre-assembled, and does not need your help, thankyouverymuch. Gato Supreme will spend most of its time in another room, curled up, sleeping. Do not disturb when it is in nap mode. Do provide scritches, pets, clean litter box, and warm laps as needed. There is no reason to be concerned when to provide these, as Gato Supreme will let you know when these are required. Feed twice daily, can be dry or wet food, but will lean towards whatever is most expensive. Routine maintenance includes a visit to the veterinarian, which can feel cost prohibitive but is necessary. Gato Supreme is not fond of routine maintenance.

WARNING: Do not rub belly, even if exposed, and do not immerse in water.

In short bursts, Gato Supreme will run or gallop at high speeds, in all directions, for no particular reason. This is normal. Gato Supreme will see and hear things you cannot, usually late at night, while you are reading Stephen King, or watching a scary movie. Gato Supreme will meow and touch your face with a paw or wet nose, to verify you are awake and alive. Gato Supreme believes it is the King or Queen of all it surveys. If you believe it too, everything will be fine.

YIELD: One happy household, for an average of 7-12 years.

WARNING: Do not purchase more than five Gato Supremes at any one time to avoid a certain reputation in your neighborhood.

Congratulations, and enjoy your Gato Supreme!

FROM THE MAKERS OF CANINE COMPANION!

*James Rodgers*

## MY CAT

My cat enjoys the wintertime
and even the fall and spring
but she doesn't like the summertime
as the heat is not her thing

So, I'll pull out my great big fan
and she smiles like it's her friend
She wishes it would play more
but she sure does love the wind

*Maggie Bowyer*

# HOW TO RECOGNIZE A WITCH

*—after Laura Jean and Elizabeth Willis*

First, follow the cackles of community and the cracks
of kindling crumbling under the combustion of our
instructions. Search for the sprite with ash on their face,
wax dripping down their fingertips, who is muttering
something unintelligible while you try to vie for their
attention. Take note of the cauldron in the corner, the
stacks of candles sorted by color and length, the smell
of wassail permeating the space. Pet their cat until you
become familiar, let your eyes linger on bookshelves
bursting with leather-bound binders, wonder about the
wine bottles brimming with sand, wait by the herb garden
in the window. Fall in love while watching their head fall
back to marvel at the moon. Spend forever wondering
which one of you cast the spell for your soulmate.

*Ronda Piszk Broatch*

## IN THE DREAM I'M DINING ON THE PATIO WITH SOME FAMOUS POETS

and my cat has just eaten one
of the pygmy elephants I shelter

in a well-appointed sanctuary
in the yard. A shy poet slips me

secretly a highly enjambed
confessional about her lover,

his affairs, how the media ripped
open his sonnets, caught him

with his pantoums
down around his ankles.

My cat is caught in the deceit.
I pull her free, and she chokes,

coughs up an earthworm, a villan-
elle, two tiny white tusks.

*Michael Magee*

## DORIAN GREY

Prowls the neighborhood late at night
looking at his reflection in the window,
shrinks from sight, his shadow, grey
with white paws, a trail of London Fog

That clothes him just a whiff of cat cologne
a sense of *dangereuse*, a velvet curse
his glassy eye sees through itself
to the other side of wonderment.

Out at night, a bowl of milk, late-night
snacks among the neighborhood riff-raff
catch-as-catch-can, or can't who can deny
the nine lives he's spent, trying to escape

his fate as Dorian Grey will never rest
until he's found and lost himself at last.

*Michael Magee*

## MR. CANNOLI, CALICO CAT

Black and white Calico—
a fur-collar wrap around his neck
like the spiral nebula itself.

Walks on the right side
of the street, every doorway
a nook and cranny to nap-in-the-sun.

The accountant keeps track of him
The Toy Store, *Tricky's*,
with treats and handouts.

Every planter a sandbox with
the warm smell of urine,
and every flower a friend.

To whoever's listening in—
a kind word, a helping hand,
cat's collar, black and white socks.

Mr. Cannoli, a touch of the poet
keeps his feet dry, counts his blessings
one mouse at a time.

*Marc Alan Di Martino*

## WILD

Some bone in you still smolders, twitching wild
each time a shadow flickers or a bird
takes flight, alights. The trees here are on fire
with life. Today it was the neighbors' ruddy
tomcat lapping water from a cistern
of glistening terracotta. Minutes passed
without a quiver in your muscles, eyes
reduced to pinpoints, marbled apertures.
Perhaps you were just curious, envious
at that cat's primal state. Hopelessly trapped
in our puzzling domestic universe
of countertops and toilet seats, throw pillows,
odoriferous human clothes, what room
is left for wildness? Can processed tuna
compete with the evolutionary grit
of tearing flesh from still-convulsing limbs?
It took millennia to tweak your genes,
domesticate the goddess in your soul
to make you—in a word—companionable
as fine statuary. Each room you dwell in
becomes a Louvre of ruthless vanity,
plush dark chamber of alien secrecy.
You stretch and galaxies unravel. Paw
and tail assess the gravitational pull
of a windowsill. To jump, or not to jump?
That is the question in your mind right now.
Three billion years of evolution meow.

*Tonia Kalouria*

## ONE FELINE FATE: Two Perspectives

Claude Cat relished scratching! He would rip things to
    shreds:
Velvet couch, lacy drapes, job reports, and brass beds.
Claude Cat adored leaping! He would spring to great
    heights,
shedding fur on Gram's goblets, laptops, and hot pipes.
Claude Cat was macho! He would howl/yowl and yell it—
then spray *Eau de Claude* far and wide so you'd smell it!

So there you have glimpsed happy-cat's bird's-eye view—
till the humans cry "WHOA! Claude's Tomfoolery won't do!"
"Incorrigible cat! We must fix him 'for good'!"
Now, forlorn-de-clawed-Claude just feels "misunderstood."
Also, in Full Disclosure, and painful to say,
once-proud, perky-Claude shed his "Tom-hood" that day.

Dejected-Claude's droopy: *ADIEU!* feline fervor.
*ALLÔ!* day-long catnaps on the shredded old berber.
Grounded-butter-pawed Claude's become oafish, a clod,
why, to get him to move takes both catnip *and* prod!
But let's take a deep dive on the bright, ***human*** side:
Claude's still got a good home, and he's had a great ride.
Sure, the foiled-feline's lazy. Of course! Life's a bore!
—But that fat tummy's useful! It *Roombas* the floor.

*Lora Berg*

## SHOOING TOMS

Like dusky sunflowers, they ring our house.
I never knew before they lived so near.
Each window I look out, one rises up,
now tawny, now smoke, torsos too muscled
for slim legs, this prowling chorus of
flea-ridden Toms. I step into the garden,
clocking the moon of their ascent.
Why be surprised? Mare drips, sow swells,
cat's supersonic tail jets up; it's time.
They are calling for my kitten. If only
they could speak to me, they'd say
they just want to make friends. I shoo them
with a broom. I lock the gates. Part of me
wants to see them leap this cinder barricade,
let them enter, let her escape, but I don't.

*Linda Conroy*

## CHOOSING FAMILY

Ernie cried the whole way home,
tiny squeaks and aching howls. A cat,
unable to explain, he crouched in the corner
of the carrier, trundled over backroads
of his former life. His past unknown

Jenny stroked his head
with one light finger—to no avail—he wailed.
At his new house he hid. Seeing his tail twitch
behind the couch, she lay and whispered to him,
gave food and toys and quiet.

Minnow purred, secure
in habits of this family; she ate and slept
and played, waiting day by day 'til, late at night,
all light being dimmed, Ernie crept out
and curled up next to her.

*Kersten Christianson*

## BOUQUET

Like an April rain song,
the girl wakes in a quiet house,
gathers her cat, curls like a shell
under her quilt with a book
she can't put down.

The weary blues of alarm clocks,
of 9 to 5, of running here and there
dissipate. It does not take a genius
child to recognize the slower pace
of a jukebox love song.

Life is fine on the summer side
of a school year. There are no
bad mornings. Dream variations
ebb and flow like the tides
of a calm sea.

*Brendan McBreen*

## kittens

kittens think
the world
their play thing
and they are right

kittens nap
as if napping
were a divine gift
and they are right

kittens will love you
just because you are there
for a kitten
just existing
makes you worthy of love

except of course
if they think
you might be edible

Henriëtte Ronner-Knip, *Primer Part II*

*Lucia Owen*

## FERAL CAT IN WINTER

O scruffy scraggly
bird murderer
suet stealer

perfect prowler
iron-pawed
terminator

winter woods
whacker of early-waking
chipmunks

O coyote snack.

*Robert Fillman*

## CAT SITTING FOR MY
## MOTHER-IN-LAW

*I left a key in the rock*
*beside the Blessed Mother*
*that overlooks my garden*
she whispered into the phone,
her meek voice skinning itself

like the fabled shroud as if
she half expected Mary
to hop on the line herself,
verify this secret. Yet

when I found the hidden key,
time slowed, the cat already
staring from the window, staked
as in a stone cross, its big
bronze eyes like torches leading
me toward the townhouse tomb.

And in the flickering dark,
a fortune of clarity,
the steel opener gouging
a perfect cylindrical
gash in the can, the wet splat
of flesh in the feline's dish,
a halo of pooled gravy,

the animal's purr winding
around me like a prayer,
still lifting me gently long
after I locked the temple,
stored the key safely away.

*Jane Alynn*

## MY CATS TAKE THE BIRDS
## FOR GRANTED

Look at them. Two cats,
fat purses, on the window seat,
unfazed by the lot of small birds
that hop around winter's
wont-withered garden,
pecking the played-out soil,
the long-spent seedpods.
Distracted with hunger
these feathered beggars would be
an easy catch for a creature
whose instincts were still intact.
But my cats have sunk into laziness.
So full of entitlements
as though they own the lap
of luxury, these soft felines
with their limitless mealtimes
yawn at the very notion
of working for supper
or feasting on anything but
a bird in the hand, canned
pâté of chicken
on their whiskered faces.

*K. L. Johnston*

## GREY CAT WITH SHADOWS

On top of the wall, camouflaged
in shadows, the grey cat waits, stares
skyward, muscles tight. The only
movement is the tail's tip, *twitch, twitch*.

Then come silhouettes overhead
and the long leap,
the blade of silvered body one
perfect cyma curve, an argent
scythe snatching the singing bird from
its element before landing
on four soft paws.

The wing tip beats, scribing a glyph
on the earth. All songs are silenced
for a moment.
The cat glances skyward once more
before melting into shadows
with his prey. Here is a lesson
of cats and birds.

The birds rise up singing again,
soft cautious notes.

*Moira Magneson*

## HIT & MISS

Our black cat Orpheus has been hit
by a car. Tail pulverized, it hangs
behind him, a thin slack rope.
Eerily calm, he hunkers below
the piano, folded shadow on a white
towel stained with blood & piss.
Tuesday, he's scheduled for amputation.
*He won't miss it* soothes the vet.
Though I'm grateful for his life,
her proclamation is plain wrong. The part
of him that is exultant signifier—
switch of anger, self-comforting embrace,
high salute of happiness—will be gone.
Of course it will be missed. A cat
is his tail. His tail his song.

*Karen Keltz*

## A FELICITOUS FELINE SCENE

15 birds perch on the yew.
Some mornings the bush sings.
I purr.
What else can an old cat do,
so full of memories and creaking bones,
but hum along, lick his paws,
switch his tail
and dream of when
the jump was easy,
the paw was swift?

*Kristy Gledhill*

## LIFE OF THE LAKE

The morning swallows
(same as the night swallows),
fresh from their power line perches,

skim through lake steam, wheel into
yards, silent bug-snatchers dodging
the ducks, who trail bobbling babies, lead
them into the weeds at the bottom

of the yard, where they doodle around
in the blackbird-topped reeds, transfixing
the cat, to whom the wrath of the mallards
is known and its memory fresh,

so he keeps his distance,
yellow-eyed
and still to the tail.

Caroline Ellen Clark, *Crouching Cat*

Nancy Canyon

## MY NOCTURNAL HUNTER

The moon is full: barred owls,
mice, and guileless possums
navigate through shadow light.
These nights, my cat's white-mittened
paw tics the back door—
I wake and rise to open it.
He darts across the yard,
ducks beneath the fence,
runs off to wherever he hunts—
perhaps the pond with its cattails,
bullfrogs, raccoons, and beaver.
With marauding coyote packs,
death's always a possibility.
I know this, yet there is no stopping
him. I cannot hold him back—
his feline life driven by instincts.
Night after night he returns,
mouse or rat clamped in strong jaws.
His yowls at the door wake me.
Wet and full of bluster, littered
with reed and rhizome, black
fur blending with the night,
he drops his prize on the doorstep
and disappears back into the dark.

*Chris Dahl*

## SWISS CATS

It's autumn in every particular
but name. Over the omnipresent peaks
a pale winter begins to rise. The cats feel lean
skies gathering.

Swiss and haughty, they staff
the fog-swagged hedges.
Their glares shame those paltry tourists,
fresh from the Low Country where even
the mice have eased indoors.

One gray tabby, harvesting
voles, appears particularly disdainful—
she'll have no truck with holiday frivolity.

Every meadow contains its working cat.
Small in a large world, they marshal their way,
leveraging intimate knowledge
to master weakness. They practice
patience and have come to terms
with service.

Those who will not work
are despised. Those who work alone,
flexing their claws,
prefer it that way.

*Steve Potter*

## TWO SONNETS IN MEMORY OF SAVAGE KNUCKLEHEAD THUNDERLORD POTTER THE FIRST AND ONLY

I.

The tiger-striped cat crouched low on the lawn
blindsides a gray mouse with a roundhouse swat.
The stunned mouse, as if asleep on its paws,
meanders through grass blades, a barroom sot,

as the cruel young cat circles around,
a bar fight favorite playing to the crowd,
and pounces and pins the mouse to the ground
and bites off its head victorious, proud.

Sitting on the porch watching this scene,
my murderous cat with her victim's head,
I realize her cruelty is mere routine,
that living for her means making things dead.

She comes rubs my leg with a meow and a purr
and licks the blood from her striped gray fur.

## II.

The collar with bells I strapped around her neck
drove her plain crazy; she ran from the yard.
Next day she was back, the collar was wrecked,
the bells were missing and her cheek was scarred.

She must have rubbed at the base of a fence
for hours on end until she was free
from the bells that warned birds at her expense
and ruined her beloved killing spree.

Before I managed to bell her again,
beheaded mice were found at the door,
a dead sparrow turned up back in the den
and if I'd searched I'd have surely found more.

To stalk, pounce, hunt would endlessly thrill her,
my warm, sweet, cute, cold-blooded mass killer.

_Judith H. Montgomery_

## POUNCE

_In which the Guest Poet Considers
Beautiful Bungee the Resident Cat_

O Mouse-Mouth, Killer Kitty, who has brought
    to my bare feet a dead curled velvet creature,
how can I think to pet your ginger fur, and not also
    how to keep my fingers far from your practiced
teeth and paws, their useful and retractable and
    unrepentant claws?
                  O Green-Eyed Glommerer-
In of wee gray bodies, Seducer of Human Hearts, you
    start your motor up the minute I've snatched
gingerly away this prize, your token gift laid out
    on the mat—I scoop him up in plastic before
you, O Connoisseur, can crouch again to gnaw
    that tiny skull.
           Dear Motor-Mouth, Hum-Heart,
I am helpless to refuse you—come, curl here
    on the couch by me, I'll stroke your belly, rub
your fuzzy skull, and praise the god who made me
    so much bigger than a mouse.

141

*Kristen McHenry*

## LIFE WITHOUT CAT

Gutter diablo, lady of trash-bones and
rag-moon eves, rabble acrobat of balustrades,
lithe warm body on bread-gold earth, soft
sack on the heft of my thighs: Gone
are our noonday naps in the lull of honey and amber.
But see, I make it through. Who are you without me
across the lyric mists? How do you mourn me?
Where do you hunt in the lands I cannot fathom?

What I did for you, I made a list: Hushed
your little cat sassies, ground your meds in filet-o-fish.
All you showed me was Theory of Theft, Parmesan
    heists, how
to win a street fight. Then also how to die,
primly and in the right order. Carry
your body up the mountain and farewell. How
you get along without me I don't know. Noonday
naps are slate and void. Frigid are these bones that held you.

# Kristen McHenry

## BASTET

I have called upon you as my blessed.
I divine our glory in the burgeoning grain,
Sing down the sun to exult the harvest
And slaughter the vermin of the fields.
In each house, bread and beer shall overflow.
I am a servant of Egypt, joyous and benevolent.

My most precious, I rise benevolent.
Loving guardian of our sacred blessed,
I prophesy the Nile's overflow
To summon the barley, flax, and grain
And call forth papyrus in the fields.
I hunt to keep the rodents from the harvest

And look with sanctity upon each harvest.
Ra my Father, most benevolent,
I shield from the serpents in the fields
Your crops kissed by ocher warmth, blessed
Nourishing fruit, abundant sorrel grain.
Every bowl be filled, and every pantry overflow.

As so the Nile, your hearts do overflow
With thanksgiving for the life-sustaining harvest,
The canals that drench the holy seeds of grain,
The silt that nurtures every seed, the benevolent
Amun, whose sacred temple stores the blessed
Surplus from the teeming, fertile fields.

Worship me as the guardian of fields
And your homes will flourish and overflow
With moon-fat children, robust and blessed

To aid in the sowing and the harvest.
I grant you my blessing for lives benevolent,
That the waters of heaven ever drench the grain.

It is I who guard the abundant grain
And at dusk loom over the honeyed fields,
Proud in spirit and benevolent
To witness the lands of Egypt overflow
With this tawny sea of harvest,
All that you may ever-thrive, my blessed.

In witness my spirits overflow
With fervor for you and for the harvest,
Perpetually devoted to my blessed.

*Deborah Woodard*

## CORSETS: AN ELEGY FOR MY CAT JEFFREY

Nervous, but never eager to admit to nerves,
I almost missed the corset shop, already bathed
in the gloom of long ago. Sifting through my pocket,
I found the minced viscera of tissues like a ticket
of admission. Something had to happen. *A. Simon*

began the legend on the door. The rest was hidden
by a flounce—a cloud the mind worked with.
I imagined glass-eyed tippets women let slide
into their laps, after a covert fumble with the clasp.
Ears and paws heaped up, softly bumping.

Because I admired her always interesting life,
I'd given a friend better than one can buy:
turn-of-the-century French stays. In exchange
she offered me a cat crying in a box, like some toy
I could poke in the mock diaphragm for sound.

Creatures equally undone by sentiment,
the half-mannequins came out to greet me
in their pelts of outmoded finery, their rosettes—
one below the bust, one setting off the neck
and diverting attention from the missing head.

Is mourning a corset, fashioned to constrain
the too permissive mind? Is regret an hourglass
intent on turning itself over? In a side window
I made out bare slats, like little sleds or the start
of fences. Something a cat would understand to leap.

*Martha Silano*

## THE CATS OF PEARL STREET

snooze in driveways, prefer
to lounge atop a neighbor's
Hyundai nicknamed *Blue*

*Angel*. They might seem
serene or lazy,
but not to the rats.

Nacho can reduce
a husky to tears
with just one hiss.

Triumphantly, I've
more than once rescued
a Bewick's wren from

Enchilada's mouth.
On Seattle's hottest day
ever, Taco ran

from a coyote
to the top of a telephone pole,
rode in a cherry picker

down to the lawn where
he sniffed the cool, evening air,
oblivious.

When the earthquake hits,
when the asteroid strikes,
I won't expect to find

all three cowering
under a porch but
raising glasses of port,

dining on Fussy Cat,
blinking away frenzied gnats.
They will outlive us.

Martha Silano

## MY CAT NACHO VERSUS THE
## TEMPERATURE OF A BLACK HOLE

I'm grateful, when I'm reading a book about the cosmos,
that Nacho's nestling against my neck,
that I can feel her toasty body

as I learn the temperature of a black hole
is ten to the minus eighth power,
*very close to absolute zero;*

as I learn that this is the temperature of a standard-sized
black hole, but that those a billion times larger
are a billion times colder;

as I learn nothing in the natural world is this cold,
that there are places, such as a black hole's
singularity—a place of infinite density

where time stops—where the temperature is ten-billionths
of a degree above minus 273 degrees Celsius—colder
than intergalactic or interstellar space;

as I Google words like *wormhole*, I'm grateful for my
        cat Nacho,
lounging beside me on this non-entangled comforter,
for her near-silent purr, her non-paradoxical warmth.

*Marge Piercy*

## The daily struggle

What is more manipulative
than your cat wanting treats?
They make loving eye contact
They rub against your legs

purring like miniature machines.
They give little pitiful mews.
They stalk around sulking,
angry cats wherever you look.

How can I resist? I must.
We don't want huge sausages
with fur, round as full moons,
dragging bellies as they walk.

No, I will be firm. I'll resist.
I swear I will… Okay, just one….

*Marge Piercy*

## They call it hampering

Stop banging on that keyboard
says Shaman the half grown kitten.
Love me, pet me, hold me. My
purr is continuous as breathing.

Am I not prettier than any poem?
Nothing on your silly computer
can love you back the way I do.
I am the cuddler staring into your

eyes, kneading your shoulder
so give up this silliness of words
and speak with your hands to me.
What you give me, I give back.

## Bethany Reid

# CATS HAVE MORE FUN

*from the painting of the same name by*
*Judith Heim*

Cats do have more fun,
dressed in tuxedos and calico,
splashing us with their Cheshire Cat grins.
Their whiskers: pure Snidely Whiplash.
Their paws: not to be trusted.
Notice it's the sexiest girl
who wears a cat costume to the party.
Whose birds are those and what is
this catbird seat everyone sits in?
Unlike the wild rabbit nibbling
your lettuce leaves, the cat
doesn't stoop to vegetables, eyes you
as if you are meat.

*Bethany Reid*

## WORRY

leaps to the bed, prances
across your legs, nips
at a flea. Worry licks a paw
and wipes its face. Green
eyes catch the light.
Worry stretches, soaks
up your heat, purrs a dirge,
kneads its talons into you
when you try to sleep.

*David D. Horowitz*

## CHAI

*—for a friend's Siamese cat*

Chai
Is shy
And while neighbor dogs might bark and woof,
Chai sits upon her owner's roof
Silent as the stars.
Chai
Loves sky
And while neighbor dogs might woof and bark,
Chai sits below the starry dark
On the gabled roof,
A bit aloof.

Ronda Piszk Broatch. *Cat on a Roof*

*David D. Horowitz*

## DISTINGUISHED

> —*for editors of dictionaries and encyclopedias*

You help distinguish lynx from lion, purr
From murmur, kit from cat, and coat from fur.
Maine Coon is not a Persian. Ocelot
Sports dotty coat, and Manx might boast a spot,
But Korat doesn't. Tigers boast a stripe;
The Yankees, lots. Ball one! But then a strike.
So, each is one, but all are not alike.
Each Jaguar is distinct, though of a type.

*Susan Rich*

## SINGING BACK THE MISSING M

This morning Miss Sarajevo
mucked up my Macintosh,

dismissing the M key

with an unambivalent purr
as she moseyed her way—

across the manmade keyboard.

Second row from the end
bottom right

one uncovered nipple must now

play the music of camembert, paramours ~
the mystical realms of the memorable

like monument and *merde!*

The upside down, the W
won't do, nor the sideways E.

Come back, come back, Miss Sarajevo!

My Madagascar companion,
O my ample female matador from Madrid—

Now words are changing into things I cannot control.

The isfits have moved on, the salmon
refurbished to salon.

My mother becomes other; her mink to only ink.

Wave good-bye to the folded road aps
of Inner Ongolia  and Western Ass.

The lights of the Editerranean at night


unable to shimmer,
they become shier.

Soon words are drifting into other worlds ~

The mountain changes to fountain,
I switch from mope to hope.

So long to the
        *ist-lit arshlands of an overly _ ired i_agination.*

I drink le_on _artinis,
help _yself to chocolate _ & _'s,

while you swig a glass of _ilk, until

*Musk melons appear in the late summer garden,*
thanks to the alchemy of you, Sarajevo.

# Priscilla Long

## CatPoem

Saturday night. My night.
I prop a slippered foot,
open notebook, poembook,
lapbook. I write: Delicious.
I write Fish. I write Ishtar.
I write the rain. My old cat—
half-Siamese, half-wild—leaps
into the poem's refrain.

The poem twitches.
It slips into sibilants
and sighs. Cardinal points of paws
dent the poem's white thighs.
It claws air, catches
crots of light, blinks
feral red eyes.

Henriëtte Ronner-Knip, *Curiosity*

*Randolph Douglas Schuder*

## DAPPLING

The brindled cow
The calico meow.
                Arc of a paw
                        Tug
                                Tilt
                              And fall.
The white-splotched rug
The spilt milk jug.

*Paulann Petersen*

## BEDMATES

My sweet white-footed witch,
I named you *Merpa* for the churr that rises
from your throat. Little tuxedo cat who wears
her blackness flared with patches of light,
you sylph into and out of my house.

No, not really my house.
Just the double-wide trailer I've come to inhabit
since my husband and his lover finished
tearing my already tattered marriage apart—
a place complete with mice
so tame, so brazen, one brushed itself
against my bare toes as I stood at the sink
washing my single plate and glass.
Hapless mice you dispatched in mere weeks
once you appeared and decided to stay.

My husband and that lover live
where I used to be at home. You and I
share this trailer, though seldom in daylight hours.
Late each night you arrive at the door,
churring the brief music of *Merpa, Merpa,*
telling me it's time to let you in.

And every night your black and white heat
curls against my face to join me in sleep.
You are my bedmate now—taking me
into the mercy of forgetfulness, waking me
into each bright-with-pain day.

My own psychopomp, you lead me—
newly dead, newly alive—back and forth between worlds.
Your warm breath flowing
inside my dreams, you teach me
animal darkness, animal light.

*Jeannine Hall Gailey*

## I USED TO THINK IT WAS ME DISAPPEARING

But it really was the world, the way it slips
away in your sleep, a shadow of what it used to be.

Didn't your friends live next door instead of in London,
weren't you just laughing about dropping out of medical
    school

to become poets? And the ocean rushing towards you at
    night,
did that part of the earth disappear as soon as you left,

the way some mountains and half of Yellowstone
have been washed away? Even if that particular bit of
sand

is gone, the ocean is just as dark and cold as that night.
I don't know how to tell you how many losses I have

counted: people I loved, homes I lived in, parts of my
    brain
I had been relying on to stay somehow steadier.

A country I had wished better than I knew it was.
Optimism at the appearance of birthday cake,

or in the sound of wings in the air? Seabirds
disappearing on our shores, in our skies,

one more fox species more or less,
have you stopped counting? I have to wrap

my arms around what is left to me, an increasingly
shrinking mass, maybe just my knees and this small cat

and a book or two, a song wavering in the background
until it, too disappears and is forgotten

*Karen Bonaudi*

## CAT TALES

*What the contrary cat
was teaching us all along.*

The only dignity in old age
is what you bring to it yourself.

Your last days are spent
like those of a Buddhist nun.
Get used to it early.

Toilet bowl water won't kill you.

Class is measured by the respect
you give to those you don't admire.

Sometimes you will be called *provocateur*
just standing your ground.

The best way to handle a nuisance
is ignore it.

Whether you realize it or not,
irony will get you every time.

When I am gone, love the dog.

No one should go the last mile alone.

In the heat of the moment,
remember what the cat taught you.

*Karen Bonaudi*

## BORIS

He has seen it all,
snow in the desert,
sunset in the mountains,
what humans do
to each other. He tolerates
tail-pulling affection,
caterwauling grandchildren,
the dog next door.
What his master needs words
to communicate, you can see
in his green eyes.

Now that his days of hunting
in the sagebrush are over,
he is content to explore
the lake bank on Sunday mornings,
amuse his humans by rolling
on olives, coughing up hairballs
and otherwise pretending
he is a cat. And at night
chase coyotes in his sleep.

*Michael Heavener*

## RITA
(Portrait in Gray and White)


Rita, tabby, gray and white, was my family's nurse. The night I had my heart attack, she laid herself tightly against my side while I slept, something she'd never done before and never did again. The next morning, I collapsed in church and spent three nights in a hospital ICU. I don't know how she knew but she did. After I recovered, she kept a watchful eye when I was in the shower and I'm sure if I slipped, she would have figured out how to get help from the rest of the family.

Cats have pointy claws
that like to find their targets;
welcome winter laps

Our grandson dropped a bit of food for the dog, but Rita got there first, apparently realizing there were other menu items than the boring dry food we gave her. From there she extrapolated that other delightful selections existed above her head in the human cafeteria. She started sitting on the chair at the far end of the table during dinner, staring daggers at us through squinting eyes in her little gray face. Then little white paws snuck their way onto the table. That led to a few shouting matches. Our blood pressure escalated—but those inscrutable eyes never wavered. We learned our manners.

Crazy as it sounds—
little feline decides
she should be the dog

I found out from Rita that cats don't always land on their feet. We lived for a while in an apartment with an open loft where I kept my computer. Rita liked to walk along the ledge on her soft white paws. One day she decided to come downstairs via the little wing wall of the refrigerator alcove instead of the stairway. She slipped and landed on her side with a hard thump. The vet said she was okay, but it really shook her up. She spent the next two years desperately trying to persuade me that the loft was not a safe place.

Son sits stroking head;
beloved cat tries her best
not to leave him alone.

*Carl Palmer*

## CALICO SENTINEL

the seedless dandelion tuft
arrives on nonexistent breeze
settling softly upon fluffy feline tail

observed by the one male kitten
in the family of four
who quickly pounces upon his prey

immediately swatted sideways
he dives for obscure safety
among his litter sisters

where he glares
at the unruffled tuft
still smugly riding mother's tail

weighing the consequence
of another of her slaps
for his certain repeat attack

*Michael Scholtes*

## LICKING THEIR FUR

Puissant pussies pretending to purr,
Abyssinians licking their fur,
Grimalkins with mittens
And alley-cat kittens
Surpass, as to class, any cur.


## PARAMOUNT MOTIVE

With their paramount motive, to munch,
Hungry "catamounts" followed a hunch.
When a tourist hiked by
With his eyes on the sky,
He was tantamount, nearly, to lunch.


* A catamount (cat-a-mountain) is a large cat of the
western U.S. also known as a mountain lion or cougar
(*Felis concolor*).

*Amy Schrader*

## THE SCHRÖDINGER ARGUMENT

When I said *sorry* I meant I'm sorry
the cat makes me so mad. He cries & cries
for food or love, which aren't the same. (In theory,
anyway.) You must admit that it defies

all logic, call it common sense: a cat
exists, is *dead // alive* until we peek
into the box. Our words are tit-for-tat.
The only proof we offer is oblique

& scientifically unsound. So if
the cat survives, it remembers only that.
To see a single life as hieroglyph
implies we must observe the other eight.

We go to bed with guns & arsenal.
Our moods change nightly (wave or particle).

*Amy Schrader*

## IDIOM

There are more ways to kill a cat
than choking it with cream. *Lactose
intolerance*, you nod, but what I meant
was poison, Geiger counter, a closed

box. We haven't spoken to each other
for days. I guess the cat has got our tongues.
We turn our backs beneath the covers
& think about our insides out: two lungs,

a xylophone of ribs, a heart. Let's not
talk about where this curiosity
will take us. In the end, it's just a thought
experiment. Our animosity

is animal, but not actually
about the cat. I love you. No, really.

*Peter Gregg Slater*

## MY CAT IS CRYING (AGAIN)

Caterwauling at 3:00 a.m.
Peak decibel.
Not getting up this time.
Taking a pass.

Every night same desolate hour.
On the dot.
Nothing physically wrong says vet.
Concluding each costly visit.
All in Tyger's head.

Jungian memories bittersweet of antelope pursuits
     across African savannas?
Yearnings for long-lost mother and siblings?
     For the flirty calico at the pet boarding?
Rage at Gulagish dinners of dry food, plain water,
     served rudely on kitchen floor?
Disgust with kitty-litter box reeking for
     a cleanse?
Guilt trip over the mice, spiders, bugs, birds
     on a long rap sheet?
Indignation at being swatted for
     clawing Persian rug?

Or does he cry and cry because he knows
how it annoys me to high heaven?
Like dealing with a bratty kid.
Who's not very bright.

*Shut the hell up*
 *or I'll come out there*
  *and really give you*
   *something to cry about!*

Stopped him cold.
Think what you will,
old-school parenting has its virtues.

_Cody Walker_

## SUNNY TANKA

She's all quick-cat, all
cat-silver. Sliver of rust,
shiv of whisker. Sand-
bagger; afterbanger. A
freeskier, but freakier.


## POEM WITH AN EPIGRAPH FROM _EDWARD LEAR, KING OF NONSENSE,_ A BIOGRAPHY FOR YOUNG PEOPLE

_"Now he felt truly alone!"_

This old man! He lived in San Remo!
And listened to nothing but emo!
His cat Foss was dead!
Of cancer, it's said!
Since nobody'd yet thought of chemo!


## THE COOL CAT SPEAKS

What's up, nerds!
I'm hunting birds.
I'm fronting raves.
I'm marking graves.

They call me kahuna!
The scourge of tuna!
Not fixed nor broken.
The cool cat's spoken.

*Issa M. Lewis*

## TEACHING CAT

My mother took night classes
at the local college. I followed
her through library shelves,
dragging my fingers along the spines,
sounding out the titles,
tongue pressed to teeth
with no sound. The air
around was heavy with knowing, trimmed
with the riffle of turning pages
and pencil scratches.
In the science section was
a dissected cat under glass,
splayed flat on its back,
paws wide in surprise or surrender.
Its now-brittle belly skin cut,
pulled back, ribcage cracked
to teach humans of lungs, stomach,
intestines, the dingy pinks
dulled by formaldehyde.
I wanted to know
if it had ever been loved,
if a warm hand had ever passed
over the white fur,
if it had ever been called
to its dinner by a name
someone chose for it. But I hid
behind my mother's legs, afraid to see
inside, what was split
wide open and vulnerable.

_Aisha Hamid_

## RESURRECTION | EARTH BABIES

_what happens to animals when they die?_
_their scores are settled_, Baba replied
_and then they become dust_
meaning I will Never meet my cats again
meaning the last time I saw them,
dead, was the Last Time I saw them
meaning Some Stories really do end. Who knew
God runs out of paper, writers run out of
heartbreaks. Cats run out of purpose
live short lives, die long deaths
like women do.

*Patricia Bollin*

## RECITAL

The family cat appears like some chemical
reaction when I play the piano, flattens
her body onto the arm of the chair,
now a calico doily, and collects
my music in her fur-tipped ears.

I am in need of being heard.

She leaves the room
with my last note and I watch
her arch her back in a satisfied stretch
as if her spine could smile at having chosen
a Bach Prelude & Fugue over television and a lap.

Henriëtte Ronner-Knip, *De Pianoles door*

## Patricia Bollin

## FUNERAL

You invited me to the funeral
for your cat. Since I knew him,
you thought I might say
a few words. Maybe write a poem.

The day was sunny, the yard festive.
The tiny cardboard coffin on the table.
No one dressed in black.
A box of Kleenex on a chair.

And so I read my poem
that told how it was for you,
this cat learned to swim,
walked on leash, held guard

at doors and windows. I drew
the details of the day you jumped—
wearing a wool coat and dress shoes—
into the deep river to save him.

Admitted I only knew him
in his suffering. Blue eyes forged
to steel, his back a rugged
mountain range of snow-capped fur.

"But he wasn't just a cat,"
I free-versed at the end, then stopped.
Those startled eyes! As if I'd
broken rank. "There's no such thing

as *just* a cat," I said. "You all know
what I mean." They did.

*Patricia Bollin*

## CAT TEAM

The cat breaks off from stalking
to glean her fur for the miscellaneous.
Even with the changed stance
she maintains an attitude.

In the world of come and go, such surety
seems so attractive. As if her daily
predictability could cure pandemics,
provide fresh answers to global warming.

It's that face, that dare-you glare that
makes you think, next she'll sit on her
haunches light up a cigar and start to
espouse planetary secrets that will save

us all. Not a stand-in for cute, her moves
have you raising your hand to be on her team.
And sure enough, next move you make
is to follow that tail through the door to dinner.

*Andrea Hollander*

## My friend tells me in a text

that his cat has stopped eating.
*She's in her last week*, he writes,
and while I am reading this,
another text chirps in: *Or last days*,
it says. I consider calling him.
I've been where he is—on the precipice
of such grief, the kind that people
who don't have pets dismiss.
Shouldn't we find a better word?
*Pets*, as if they exist only for us
to stroke their warm bodies,
welcome them onto our beds.
*But she still gives me a purr*,
the next text says, though I've yet
to answer his first. And I begin
to understand he does not need
to have even one word from me.
He taps each letter with his thumbs
or a forefinger and imagines me
on the other end, as if this
were a phone conversation
and he can hear each breath I take.
Or he imagines us sitting
side by side at our favorite café,
and he feels through his own body
the way my heart speeds up
as he speaks. And I would hear
the way his voice breaks at each
syllable. But we would not be
at the café. We'd be in his apartment
sitting cross-legged on the beige carpet,

the bright afternoon slowing down,
his cocoa-colored cat curled in his lap,
wheezing, then quieting, the two of us
not speaking, but petting and petting
her soft, still fur.

*Joannie Stangeland*

## FIRMAMENT

Sunlight was made for the cat
   or the cat was made for sunlight
stretched out on the floor.

   Saw that it was good.

Little sigh, little snore. What glory
   is a cat in the sun
that moves the cat around,
   a trick of windows rearranging rest.

Slight twitch of tail.
One eye opened.

   Saw that it was good.

The light comes in without knocking.
   The cat ages, feeling his weight,
his sleep in gravity and sunlight.

   Saw that it was good.

In a hunkering, each incursion
   of the outside world
makes a gift or a warning

as when smoke stains
   the sunlight orange or rose,
my inner alarms all day clanging.

Is it the distance or my heart,
the losses and smoldering?

Oh, for that fluffy body
    to sprawl along the day until
he is nudged by other hungers.

    See that it is good:
the splay of cat, the time for light.

## Joannie Stangeland

## JUBILATE MEDIA NOCTE

*—after Christopher Smart*

For he announces his presence with authority.
For his voice can surely wake the dead.
For we feel next to dead when he yowls us from sleep.
For we know not what he needs.
For he knows not what he needs.
For he has eaten his common portion twice over.
For he has found the loudest place in the house.
For he licks our ears and bites our noses.
For he kneads our necks with his claws.
For he comes to the bed smelling of his recent shit.
For what goes in must come out.
For anything is food to him and sometimes sticks
in his gut. For he has been cut open
five times to remove what is not food. For to him
it looked like sustenance or felt good chewing.
For he has conquered the kitchen counters
and will consume whatever is not shut in the cupboard.
For he has mastered the door to the garbage and proves
his worth by strewing trash through the house.
For he jumps on the mantle to show his agility.
He is not agile, but he is a prideful cat.
For he fetches the ball and asks us to throw it again.
For the ball is loud in the darkness.

*Joannie Stangeland*

## OH, KITTY BUDDY

I remember Gilbert playing fetch, patting the catnip
    mouse closer, so I could throw it again.

I remember batting practice, Gilbert leaping like a
    gymnast, then waiting for me to fetch and pitch again.

I remember games of tag, Gilbert chasing me through the
    house, or racing, "making a vacuum."

I remember Gilbert stretching out, "sausaging" long on
    the rug.

I remember his fluffiness, and the white spot on his back
    like someone spilled the paint.

I remember Gilbert watching birds through the window,
    saying *gnyack, gnyack, gnyack, gnyack.*

I remember Gilbert launching himself at my shoulder as I
    climbed the stairs.

I remember the sound of Gilbert walking downstairs—
    like an elephant!

I remember Gilbert gathering all his toys by the back door
    to greet us when we came home.

I remember him "being a dog," sprawling on the floor near
    Tom as he read the morning paper.

I remember Gilbert perched on the easy chair arm, waiting
for Tom to settle in for evening cuddling.

I remember Gilbert getting into the garbage.

I remember Gilbert opening cupboard doors because he
could.

I remember Gilbert leaping onto the bed in the morning to
be family with us.

I remember him curling by my feet, or climbing up to my
chest, and purring me to sleep.

He was "the somnambulator."

I remember, recently, Gilbert pawing at my leg, asking to
be lifted to my lap.

The good parts and the hard parts, Gilbert, I remember.

*Joannie Stangeland*

## THE CAT'S POEM

Waiting for snow to write the branches, grass, mud into
　　a poem.

The day stays as gray as the cat who appeared last night.

The cat as gray as a ghost hunched on our front porch.

More fluff and purr than body, waiting to make our house
　　his home.

A place left bare after our cat died.

The night was cold and colder.

Snugged close to the storm door—still, he stayed.

This gray cat with collar, tags, a name and numbers.

Maybe Lenny was lost or missing? The cat's poem,
　　*I am here and don't know where.*

My son texted the owners, who were out of town.

Could we take him to their house, let him in? and we did.

How strange the cat choosing our house, and strange the
　　staying.

This morning, I check the porch, hoping, knowing it's
　　wrong.

*Joannie Stangeland*

## LINES WRITTEN WHILE KITTENS NAP
## ON MY LAP

Thin string, anything
that dangles, the bathrobe belt,
the cord for the blinds, a coat
draped over a chair,
the air roots hanging
spindly from the orchid on the sill.
Anything that moves—leaf
shadows flit-shivering
on the rug, a hand writing,
another cat's tail.
Anything that might tumble
or roll—a wine cork
from last night, that squat
glass vase on the mantle.
Scratch paper crumpled
becomes a snowball,
or twist it into a butterfly—
tied to twine, it flies!
A teddy bear left
behind by the human children,
a leaf tracked in on someone's
sneaker, and the laces! Their taste
of outside and the fingers that tied them.

*Joannie Stangeland*

## AUTUMN TIDE

The word "tide," I learn, first meant time
and later water. High times and low.

Surging into the room, the kittens I wanted
storm the house, their new world to conquer.

I wanted the kittens for purr tide,
quiet tide. A philosopher said

the hardest thing is to know what you want.
No. The hardest is to know who I am.

I return to Woolf's novel, morning,
Lily at the table, feeling nothing.

I will call my feelings and try to name them
when I visit my mother who must learn,

again, the courage to walk, to navigate
each step across the linoleum.

Played out for now, the kittens sleep, sprawled
on the sofa—at the smallest noise, they shift,

stretch, drift back to napping, resting up
to wreak and relish more havoc.

The kittens rest up for more chase and wrestle.
My mother rests from ninety years of living.

At the transitional care unit, she swims
through sleep until she stirs, and I greet her.

It's not that she doesn't know me,
but that she has not surfaced fully.

She plucks words from the haze
of waking, the half-speech of still-dreaming,

navigates between the two worlds.
Is it cruel to insist on this one?

I hold an ocean behind my eyes.
I thought that kittens would solve everything,

this emotional vertigo, the high wave
breaking, sucking me under.

The tide rises, slacks, ebbs, and again.
Imagine sunlight on the water, somewhere.

"Autumn Tide" and "Held" are part of a series that's
in conversation with Virginia Woolf's novel *To the
Lighthouse*, and the mentions of "Lily" refer to Woolf's
character Lily Briscoe.

*Joannie Stangeland*

## HELD

One kitten curled on the sofa,
one kitten sprawled on the rug,

then teeth on fingers, attacking the pen.
Life is to be lived, not written.

The sun halos the tallest trees
as it passes. September, the season

for beginnings and endings.
Harvest as both abundance and death.

I reap the moments I can.
*What is the meaning of life?*

When Lily thinks it's a simple question,
I falter, flooded by my disbelief.

True, I had not considered
the quotidian flow as a stream

of miracles, small bubbles stringing
into a single moment of grace.

In Woolf's novel, tide lapping, shell crunch
and gravel under foot, wind snatching laughter,

the *swit, swit* of stones skipping. I turn
from her harbor, drift closer to this life.

Always much to be done.
Much to be misunderstood, or missed.

The miracle of my mother's hands
on her blanket while she sleeps.

*Doug Stone*

## ODE TO JACK

He slept the deep, good sleep of the gods,
bathed in the warm praise from the sun
that knew it existed only for his pleasure.

His purr strummed the air with the song
of his contentment as he dreamed of small
things twitching between his paws.

He woke, aware the world needed him,
licked the sweet marrow of sun from his fur,
then punished the recalcitrant sofa with his claws.

He strolled through the dull atmosphere of the house
without judgment or mercy, and blessed
the uninteresting rooms with his elegance.

He was always a creature of the moment,
and what a magnificent moment he was.

Henriëtte Ronner-Knip, *St. Nicholas series*

# ACKNOWLEDGMENTS

We gratefully acknowledge previous or forthcoming publications:

Kelli Russell Agodon: The epigraph to "Surrealist Women Grow(l)ing from Lemon Trees" originally appeared at the beginning of "Fruit Salad Body," an essay in the "Branches" section of *Fruitflesh: Seeds of Inspiration for Women Who Write* by Gayle Brandeis (Harper San Francisco/Harper Collins, 2002).

Jane Alynn, "My Cats Take the Birds for Granted," *Necessity of Flight* (Cherry Grove Collections, 2011)

Lana Hechtman Ayers: "The Shovel," forthcoming in *The Autobiography of Rain* (Fernwood Press, 2024)

Margaret Chula: "Tanka," *Perigee Moon* (Red Mountain Press, 2021)

David Denny: "Flea Meds," *Fool in the Attic* (Kelsay Books/Aldrich Press, 2013); "Suburban Scene," *Canary* and *Some Divine Commotion* (Shanti Arts, 2017)

William Dunlop: "Old Tom," "The Lion's Share," *Caruso for the Children, & Other Poems* (Rose Alley Press, 1997) and *Collected Poems* (Classic Day Publishing, 2007)

Victoria Ford: "The Caracal," *Following the Swan* (Fireweed Press, 1988)

Michael Fraley: "The Cat," *The Road Not Taken;* "The Old Lion," *Poets' Espresso Review*

Benjamin S. Grossberg: "The Next World," *My Husband Would* (University of Tampa Press, 2020)

Jack Harvey: "Cats," *Scarlet Leaf Review*

Sharon Hashimoto: "Bus Stop at Hanapepe," *The Crane Wife* (Story Line Press, an imprint of Red Hen Press, 2021)

Andrea Hollander: "My friend tells me in a text," *And Now, Nowhere But Here* (Terrapin Books, 2023)

David D. Horowitz: "Chai," *The Lyric*

Brendan McBreen: "kittens," *The Memory of Water* (MoonPath Press, 2021)

Susan McLean: "The Panther," translation of Rainer Maria Rilke's "Der Panther," *Peacock Journal;* "The Cat," translation of Charles Baudelaire's "Le Chat," *Transference*

James B. Nicola: "Nephew and Cat," *Lips;* "Waking Up to Cat," *Greensilk Journal*

Carl Palmer: "Calico Sentinel," *The Feline Muse, Senior Scene* and *Old Mill Road*

Randolph Douglas Schuder: "Dappling," *To Enter the Stillness* (Rose Alley Press, 2000)

Michael Spence: "Move and Countermove," *Willow Springs*

Timothy Steele: "For Kashmir," *First Things;* "The Mountain Lion of Central Park," *Able Muse*

Jean Syed: "The Cat and the Lion," *Footbridge Above the Falls: Poems by Forty-Eight Northwest Poets*, edited by David D. Horowitz (Rose Alley Press, 2019)

Alarie Tennille: "*When the teacher is ready, the pupil will come.*," *I-70 Review*

Richard Wakefield: "Contemplation," *Many Trails to the Summit: Poems by Forty-Two Pacific Northwest Poets*, edited by David D. Horowitz (Rose Alley Press, 2010)

Cody Walker: "Poem with an Epigraph from *Edward Lear, King of Nonsense*, a Biography for Young People," *The Self-Styled No-Child* (The Waywiser Press, 2016)

Gayle White: "Abelard, or Love Gone Wrong," "Cat Hoarder," "Fat Cat," "Saint Francis Preaches to the Cats, Who Pay No Attention," "The Solitary Woman," *Catechism* (White Violet Press, 2016)

Deborah Woodard: "Corsets: An Elegy for My Cat Jeffrey," *Artful Dodge*

Tachibana Morikuni, *Domestic cat nursing kittens*

# ABOUT OUR CONTRIBUTING AUTHORS

**Carolyn Adams'** work has appeared in *Steam Ticket, Cimarron Review*, and *Evening Street Review*, among others. She is the editor and publisher of the Oregon Poetry Calendar. Her full-length volume is forthcoming from Fernwood Press. She has been nominated for both Best of the Net and a Pushcart Prize.

**Kelli Russell Agodon's** newest book, *Dialogues with Rising Tides* (Copper Canyon Press), was a Finalist in the Washington State Book Awards. Kelli cofounded Two Sylvias Press, where she is an editor and book cover designer. She teaches at Pacific Lutheran University's low-res MFA program, the Rainier Writing Workshop. www.agodon.com / www.twosylviaspress.com

**Jane Alynn**, poet and photographer, is the author of *Necessity of Flight* and *Threads & Dust*. Her most recent award was Second Place in *New South's* 2012 Poetry Contest. Her poems have appeared in numerous journals and anthologies; those written in collaboration with visual artists have been exhibited in galleries.

**Lana Hechtman Ayers** has published over a hundred poetry volumes as managing editor for three small presses. Her work appears in *Rattle, The London Reader, Peregrine, The MacGuffin*, and other journals. Visit her online at LanaAyers.com.

**Tom Barlow** is an Ohio writer of poetry, short stories, and novels. His work has appeared in journals including *They Said, Trampoline, Ekphrastic Review, Voicemail Poetry, Hobart, Tenemos, Redivider, The North Dakota Quarterly, The New York Quarterly, The Modern Poetry Quarterly*, and many more. Visit tombarlowauthor.com.

**Charles Baudelaire** (1821–1867), in his brooding collection *Les Fleurs du Mal* (*The Flowers of Evil*), brought intensity and perversity to his poems of urban life. (bio by Susan McLean)

**Sheila Bender** founded WritingItReal.com and has authored instructional books on writing personal essays, poetry, and keeping a writer's journal. Her newest collection is *Since Then: Poems and Short Prose* from Ex Ophidia Press in Seattle. She and her husband lived with two spiritual apple head Siamese sibling cats for years.

**Betty Benson** lives and writes in Minnesota. Her work has appeared or is forthcoming in *RockPaperPoem*, *As Above So Below*, and anthologies from *Of Rust and Glass* and Muswell Press. She is known as someone who loves cats just a little bit more than is reasonable.

**Lora Berg** wrote *The Mermaid Wakes* with artist Canute Caliste. Her poems have appeared in *Shenandoah, Colorado Review*, and other publications. She served as Poet-in-Residence at St. Albans School and holds an MFA from Johns Hopkins. Lora has served as cultural attaché abroad. She is a proud mom and grandma.

More than 100 of **Laura J. Bobrow's** poems have appeared in various media, including a fourth-grade textbook in Abu Dhabi. A renaissance woman, she has had multiple careers: magazine editor, folksinger, artist. Her short stories have appeared in numerous anthologies. She is, in addition, an acclaimed professional storyteller. www.laurajbobrow.com

**Ace Boggess** is author of six books of poetry, most recently *Escape Envy* (Brick Road, 2021). His writing has appeared in *Michigan Quarterly Review, Rattle, Harvard Review*, and other journals. An ex-con, he lives in Charleston, West Virginia, where he writes and tries to stay out of trouble.

**Patricia Bollin** is a poet, retired bureaucrat, mother and grandmother. Her poetry has appeared in publications including *The Fourth River, Passager, Mezzo Cammin,* and the 2019 anthology *Footbridge Above the Falls: Poems by Forty-Eight Northwest Poets*. She serves as board president of Soapstone, an organization dedicated to supporting women's writing.

**Karen Bonaudi** has conducted readings, workshops, and writing classes, served as Washington Poets Association president, and helped establish the Washington State Poet Laureate program. Her poems have appeared in *Bellingham Review, Pontoon, Cascade Journal, Take a Stand: Art Against Hate*, and her chapbook *Editing a Vapor Trail* (Pudding House Press).

**Maggie Bowyer** (they/them/theirs) is a poet, cat parent, and the author of various poetry collections including *Allergies* (2023) and *When I Bleed* (2021). They've been published in *The Abbey Review, Chapter Journal, The South Dakota Review, Wishbone Words*, and more. You can find their work on Instagram and TikTok @maggie.writes.

**Ronda Piszk Broatch's** latest poetry collection is *Chaos Theory for Beginners* (MoonPath Press). Ronda's journal publications include *Fugue, Blackbird, 2River, Sycamore Review, Missouri Review, Palette Poetry*, and NPR News / KUOW's *All Things Considered*. She is a graduate student working toward her MFA at Pacific Lutheran University's Rainier Writing Workshop.

After being homeless in her teens, **Cathy Bryant** worked as a life model, shoe shop assistant, civil servant and childminder before writing professionally. Hundreds of her poems and stories have been published internationally, and she has won thirty-three literary awards. See Cathy's listings for impoverished writers at www.compsandcalls.com/wp.

**Nancy Canyon**, MFA, is published in Raven Chronicles' *Take a Stand: Art Against Hate, Water~Stone Review, Fourth Genre, Floating Bridge Review, Last Call, Ice Cream Poems*, and more. She teaches writing through Chuckanut Writers and coaches for The Narrative Project. Her books, *Saltwater* and *Celia's Heaven*, are available at villagebooks.com

**Elise Chadwick** lives in NYC and upstate NY. She's not really a cat person but family and friends are. Her poems have been recently published in *The Paterson Literary Review, Healing Muse, Literary Mama,* and *The English Journal*.

**Kersten Christianson** is a poet and English teacher from Sitka, Alaska. She has authored *Curating the House of Nostalgia* (Sheila-Na-Gig), *What Caught Raven's Eye* (Petroglyph Press), and *Something Yet to Be Named* (Kelsay Books). Kersten chases road trips, bookstores, and smooth ink pens. Her daughter, Rie, befriends all cats.

**Margaret (Maggie) Chula** has published fourteen poetry collections including, most recently, *Firefly Lanterns: Twelve Years in Kyoto*. She has received grants from the Oregon Arts Commission and the Regional Arts and Culture Council and fellowships to the Vermont Studio Center, Helene Wurlitzer Foundation, and PLAYA. She lives in Portland, Oregon.

**Rick Clark** is a Seattle poet, editor, educator, and UW MFA recipient who's dabbled in filmmaking, classical violin, birds, photography, Zen, and yoga. His books *Journey to the River: India Travels* and *bug-eyed & bird-brained: small creature haiku* were published in 2016. Rick is writing a partially fictionalized ancestry memoir.

**Joanne Clarkson's** sixth poetry collection, *Hospice House*, was released by MoonPath Press in 2023. Her poems have been published in such journals as *Poetry Northwest, Nimrod, Western Humanities Review,* and *Beloit Poetry Journal.* Clarkson lives in Port Townsend, Washington, with her husband Jim and tabby cat Miss Alice.

**Sheryl Clough** has worked as an Upward Bound instructor, paralegal and whitewater river guide. Her chapbook *Ring of Fire, Sea of Stone* won the 2013 San Gabriel Valley Literary Festival Competition. Numerous journals have published Sheryl's stories, poems, and nonfiction, and her photographs were featured at Chicago's Cleve Carney Museum.

**Linda Conroy**, a retired social worker, likes to write about the connection between human nature and the natural world, and to observe the changing times. She is the author of two poetry collections, *Ordinary Signs* and *Familiar Sky*.

**Chris Dahl** cups handfuls of murky pond-water, examining another world half-hidden in this one. Her chapbook, *Mrs. Dahl in the Season of Cub Scouts*, won Still Waters Press "Women's Words" competition. Extensively published, she also serves on the Olympia Poetry Network board and edits their newsletter.

**David Denny's** books include the verse collections *Some Divine Commotion* and *Fool in the Attic*. His work has appeared in *Narrative, Rattle*, and *Parabola*. Honors include The Steve Kowit Poetry Prize and numerous Pushcart Prize nominations. He and his wife Jill, a prominent choir conductor, live in California. Visit daviddenny.net.

**Marc Alan Di Martino** is the author of *Still Life with City* (Pski's Porch, 2022) and *Unburial* (Kelsay, 2019). His work appears in *Rattle, THINK* and many other journals and anthologies. His translation *Day Lasts Forever: Selected Poems of Mario dell'Arco* will be published by World Poetry Books in 2024.

**Kris Michelle Diesness** resides in Wheaton, Illinois, with her two cats, Luna and Nova, and her husband. She holds a B.A. in English: Writing Emphasis from Dominican University and an M.A. in Transpersonal Psychology from Sofia University.

**William Dunlop** (1936–2005), from Southampton, England, taught English at the University of Washington for forty years. Rose Alley Press published his collection *Caruso for the Children, & Other Poems*, and Classic Day Publishing posthumously published his *Collected Poems*. His poems appeared in *Encounter, TLS, Poetry Northwest,* and *The Seattle Review.*

**Robert Fillman** is the author of *House Bird* (Terrapin, 2022) and *November Weather Spell* (Main Street Rag, 2019). Individual poems have appeared in such venues as *The Hollins Critic, Poetry East, Salamander, Spoon River Poetry Review, Tar River Poetry*, and *Verse Daily*. He teaches at Kutztown University in eastern Pennsylvania.

**Victoria Ford** earned her MFA from Indiana University. Her chapbooks include *Following the Swan* (Fireweed Press) and *Rain Psalm* (Rose Alley Press). Other publication credits include *Petroglyph* and *Crosswinds Poetry Journal*. A former college-level English instructor, Victoria currently works as a tutor and an independent contractor for education companies.

**Michael Fraley** finds a creative community in the many voices of the poetry world. Michael and family live in San Francisco near the beach and zoo. He has contributed to *The Listening Eye, Blue Unicorn, California Quarterly, Light, Pennine Ink, The Lyric, miller's pond,* and *The Road Not Taken*.

**Jeannine Hall Gailey** is a poet with MS who served as Poet Laureate of Redmond, Washington. She's the author of six books of poetry, including her latest, *Flare, Corona*. Her work appeared in journals like *The American Poetry Review, Ploughshares*, and *Poetry*. Her website is www.webbish6.com. Twitter and Instagram: @webbish6.

When she's not writing, teaching yoga, or working for justice, **Kristy Gledhill** is playing with, cleaning up after, or laughing at her three kittens—Leo, Vindaloo, and Byrd. She creates poetry in western Washington and her work has appeared in *Terrain.org, Dunes Review, Creative Colloquy,* and *Sweet Lit*.

**Art Gomez** was born and crazed in Omaha, Nebraska, where he subjected schoolmates to bad pun cartoons: "The Further Adventures of Cliché Man." In Seattle, Washington, since 1981, he is now retired from the field of developmental disabilities. Art is a former host of *PoetsWest* at Seattle's Green Lake Library.

**Jack Granath** is a librarian in Kansas.

**John Grey** is an Australian poet, United States resident, recently published in *Sheepshead Review, Stand, Washington Square Review,* and *Floyd County Moonshine*. Latest books, *Covert, Memory Outside The Head,* and *Guest Of Myself* are available through Amazon. Work upcoming in the *McNeese Review, Santa Fe Literary Review,* and *Open Ceilings*.

**Benjamin S. Grossberg** is the author of four poetry collections, including *My Husband Would* (University of Tampa, 2020), winner of the 2021 Connecticut Book Award, and *Sweet Core Orchard* (University of Tampa, 2009), winner of a Lambda Literary Award. He directs the Creative Writing concentration at the University of Hartford.

**Sarah Das Gupta** is a retired teacher living near Cambridge, UK. Her work can be read in many online and print magazines and anthologies. She has always had a great interest in animals and lived in homes with a virtual menagerie. She has great childhood memories of Burmese cats.

**Aisha Hamid** is a feminist writer and poet based in Lahore, Pakistan. She was shortlisted by the Zeenat Haroon Rashid Writing Prize for Women, 2019. Her poetry has been published by *Vallum Magazine, The Aleph Review* and Rare Swan Press. She is a Poetry Reader at *The Adroit Journal*.

**Jack Harvey** has been writing poetry since he was sixteen and lives in a small town near Albany, New York. He is retired from doing whatever he was doing before he retired.

**Sharon Hashimoto's** *The Crane Wife* was co-winner of the 2003 Nicholas Roerich Prize and reprinted by Red Hen Press in 2021. That same year, her second collection, *More American*, won the 2021 Off the Grid Poetry Prize. *More American* went on to win the 2022 Washington State Book Award.

**J.K. Hayward-Trout** usually writes poems into tiny fissures of her fiction and fantasy writing, but she occasionally pulls a few crystalline pieces out for display on their own. She is published in the online journals *The Dewdrop, 101 Words,* and *Writing It Real.*

**Michael Heavener** writes anecdotal and humorous poetry to keep himself grounded to his roots in Washington, love of history, trains, theology, adventures, and his pets and family. Michael is treasurer of the Redmond Association of Spokenword. His poems have been published in regional anthologies and displayed as framed art.

**Andrea Hollander's** sixth full-length poetry collection, *And Now, Nowhere But Here*, was published by Terrapin Books in 2023. Her many journal and magazine publications include a recent feature in *The New York Times Magazine*. Other honors include two Pushcart Prizes (poetry and literary nonfiction) and two poetry fellowships from the National Endowment for the Arts.

**David D. Horowitz** founded Rose Alley Press in 1995, through which he has published eighteen books, including his latest poetry collection, *Slow Clouds over Rush Hour*. His poems have appeared in *Raven Chronicles, The Lyric, Terrain.org, The Literary Nest, Exterminating Angel*, and many other publications. Visit www.rosealleypress.com.

**Holly J. Hughes** is the author of four poetry collections, most recently *Hold Fast*; her chapbook *Passings* received an American Book Award in 2017. She co-publishes Empty Bowl Press, directs Flying Squirrel Studio, which offers residencies for women, and consults as a writing coach. She lives on the Olympic Peninsula.

**Christopher J. Jarmick** owns BookTree Kirkland, an independent new and gently used book store in Kirkland, Washington. Christopher is a creative and freelance writer, impresario, investigator, creator, and poet. His most recent collection is *Not Aloud* (MoonPath Press, 2015). He blogs at PoetryIsEverything.

From her home in Winona, Minnesota, **Linda Jenkinson** is a retired copywriter and commercial content writer. Since retirement, she has rediscovered her passion for poetry and story, and enjoys putting life's warts and wrinkles into slice-of-life stories and poems.

**K.L. Johnston's** poetry has appeared in literary magazines and anthologies since the 1970s. She holds a degree in English and Communications from the University of South Carolina, and her wide-ranging interests contribute to her writing. She is co-owned by two cats, Bast and Tippler.

**Barbara Johnstone's** poems appear in many publications, including *Diagram; Crosswinds; New York Quarterly Online; Persimmon Tree; Raven Chronicles; "Dirt?"* (exhibit and catalogue), University of Puget Sound; and The Nature Conservancy's "Rooted in Puget Sound" contest winners online. She misses Tourky lying on the computer while she tries to write this.

**Tonia Kalouria** is a former soap actress and teacher living near Cleveland, Ohio. She has poems in *Society of Classical Poets, Lighten Up Online, The 5-2, Take5ive, 7 Anthologies, Tigershark, Asses of Parnassus, The Whiskey Blot, Nothing Ever Happens in Fox Hollow,* and *Literary Veganism.*

**Karen Keltz** has been published in *Global Poemic, The North Coast Squid, the dillydoun review, Poésie,* and *Verseweavers,* among others. She has won awards for poetry, non-fiction, fiction, and screenwriting. Her middle-grades novel, *Laurel Hedges and the Evil Lurkers,* is available on Amazon. She lives in Tillamook, Oregon.

**Elizabeth Kerlikowske's** ninth chapbook, *The Vaudeville Horse,* was published in 2022 by Etchings Press. She works for two nonprofits, both connected to poetry. She was awarded the Community Medal for the Arts in 2017. Her work has appeared recently in *Sleet Magazine, Cloudbank, Thimble Literary Magazine,* and other journals.

**Issa M. Lewis's** books are *Infinite Collisions* (Finishing Line Press, 2017) and *Anchor* (Kelsay Books, 2022). She received the 2013 Lucille Clifton Poetry Prize. Her poems have appeared or are forthcoming in *Rust & Moth, Thimble, North American Review, South Carolina Review, Panoply,* and other journals. She lives in West Michigan.

**Priscilla Long's** books of poems are *Holy Magic* (MoonPath Press) and *Crossing Over: Poems* (University of New Mexico Press). Her most recent book (prose) is *Dancing with the Muse in Old Age*. Ten of her essays have been honored as "notable" in various years of Best American Essays. www.priscillalong.com.

**Michael Magee** has read at Shakespeare and Co., Paris, Palace of the Legion of Honor in San Francisco, on VerseDaily.org, and with the Jack Straw Writing Program. His poetry has been published in the U.K., Greece, and the U.S., and he has written for radio drama, dance, and theatre.

**Moira Magneson** calls the Sierra Foothills home and taught English for many years at Sacramento City College. Before teaching, she worked as a river guide throughout the West. Her poems have appeared in a variety of journals, including *Passager*, the *New Verse News, Persimmon Tree*, and *Plainsongs*.

**Torrey Francis Malek** is a poet and logician hailing from northern Delaware. Torrey expresses his passion through poetry, prose, and short-story fiction while covering a wide variety of subjects, centered usually on observation, family dynamics, history, and mental health, often from a humorist's perspective.

**Jayne Marek** lives a stone's throw from where the Pacific Ocean turns in toward Puget Sound. She has published six poetry collections, with her next, *Dusk-Voiced*, due in 2023. Her writings appear in *Terrain, Rattle, Spillway, Catamaran, Salamander, Bloodroot, One, Calyx, Bellevue Literary Review, About Place Journal,* and elsewhere.

**Brendan McBreen** is a poet and collage artist. MoonPath Press published their two collections: *Cosmic Egg* and *The Memory of Water*. They help lead "Striped

Water Poets," a weekly literary critique circle based in Auburn, Washington, and for years they managed the literary program at the annual AuburnFest. Visit www.transpoeticdesigns.com.

**Kristen McHenry** is a Seattle-based poet and writer. She has authored four poetry chapbooks, and her work has been seen in publications including *Busk, Tiferet, Big Pulp, Dark Matter*, and the anthology *Many Trails to the Summit*. You can follow her work on her blog, *The Good Typist,* on Substack.

**Susan McLean**, professor emerita of English at Southwest Minnesota State University, is the author of two poetry books, *The Best Disguise* and *The Whetstone Misses the Knife*, and the translator of a book of Latin poems by Martial, *Selected Epigrams*.

**Katherine Meizel** is Professor of Ethnomusicology at Bowling Green State University in Ohio. She has authored two academic books and edited another; her writing has also appeared in *Slate*, *NPR.org, The New Republic,* and *The Conversation*, as well as literary venues such as *A Plate of Pandemic* and *Kaleidoscope*.

**Shelley Minden** is a poet and storyteller in Seattle, Washington, where she's an active member of Hugo House, a center for writers. She has a chapbook called *Shape Shift* from Finishing Line Press. She misses her brown tabby, Hestia, who inspired many poems and even typed a few herself.

**Judith H. Montgomery's** poems appear in *Poet Lore, Tahoma Literary Review,* and elsewhere. Her first collection, *Passion*, received the Oregon Book Award for Poetry. Her fourth book, *Litany for Wound and*

*Bloom,* appeared in August 2018. Her prize-winning narrative medicine chapbook, *Mercy*, appeared in March 2019.

**Daniel Thomas Moran**, the former poet laureate of Suffolk County, New York, is the author of fourteen collections of poetry, the most recent being *In the Kingdom of Autumn*, published in 2020 by Salmon Poetry in Ireland. He has had close to 400 poems published in twenty different countries.

**Larry Needham** is a retired community college teacher who has published on Romantic literature and the poetry of Agha Shahid Ali. His work has recently appeared in various online journals, including: *Amethyst Review, The Alchemy Spoon, Lighten Up Online*, and *miller's pond poetry magazine*. He lives in Oberlin, Ohio.

**James B. Nicola's** seven full-length poetry collections include *Fires of Heaven* and *Turns & Twists* (2021-2022). His poetry and prose have received a Dana Literary Award, two *Willow Review* awards, one Best of the Net, one Rhysling, and ten Pushcart nominations. His nonfiction book *Playing the Audience* won a *Choice* award.

**Lucia Owen** is a retired high school English teacher living in Maine. Her work has appeared in *The Cafe Review, Rust & Moth, Prospectus, Spire: The Maine Journal of Conservation and Sustainability, A Dangerous New World: Maine Voices on the Climate Crisis*, and *Wait: Poems from the Pandemic*. Cats find her.

**Carl "Papa" Palmer** of Old Mill Road in Ridgeway, Virginia, lives in University Place, Washington. He is retired from the military and Federal Aviation

Administration (FAA), enjoying life as "Papa" to his grand descendants and being a Franciscan Hospice volunteer. PAPA's MOTTO: *Long Weekends Forever!*

**Paulann Petersen**, Oregon Poet Laureate Emerita, has eight full-length books of poetry, most recently *My Kindred*, from Salmon Poetry in Ireland. In 2022, the Latvian composer Eriks Esenvalds commissioned three poems from her to use as the lyrics in his new choral composition, *Naming the Rain.*

**Marge Piercy** has published twenty poetry collections, most recently, *ON THE WAY OUT, TURN OFF THE LIGHT* (Knopf); seventeen novels; a short story collection; and five non-fiction books. She has read at 575 venues here and abroad.

**Steve Potter's** poems have appeared in journals such as *Able Muse, Coe Review, Danse Macabre, E·Ratio, Otoliths*, and *Word/ForWord*. His book reviews may be found in *Golden Handcuffs Review, Pacific Rim Review of Books, Parole Blog of the Black Bart Poetry Society, Raven Chronicles,* and on his own blog, *BookFreak.*

**Joseph Powell** lives in Ellensburg, Washington, on a small farm. He has published seven books of poetry; the most recent is *The Slow Subtraction: ALS*, published by MoonPath Press in 2019.

**Bethany Reid's** *Sparrow* won the 2012 Gell Poetry Prize. Her latest collection, *The Pear Tree*, won MoonPath Press's 2023 Sally Albiso Award. Her work has appeared in *Poetry East, Quartet, Passengers,* and *Persimmon Tree*. Bethany and her husband live in Edmonds, Washington, near their grown daughters, and grand-cats. Visit http://www.bethanyareid.com.

**JC Reilly** is the author of *What Magick May Not Alter* and *Amo e Canto*. She has work published in or forthcoming from a number of journals, and serves as the Managing Editor of *Atlanta Review*. When not writing, she crochets, plays tennis, or practices her Italian. Follow her @Aishatonu.

**Susan Rich** is the author of seven books including *Gallery of Postcards and Maps, Cloud Pharmacy*, and *The Alchemist's Kitchen*. Her poetry has earned awards from PEN USA and the *Times Literary Supplement*. Susan's work appears in *Harvard Review, O Magazine,* and *Poetry Ireland*. She teaches at Highline College.

**Rainer Maria Rilke** (1875–1926) was one of the greatest German modernist poets. In the "thing poems" of his *New Poems* (1907 and 1908), he explored the appearances of people, creatures, and objects as a way of getting at their essence. (bio by Susan McLean)

**James Rodgers** is a Pacific Northwest poet and is the current Poet Laureate for Auburn, Washington. He lives with a wife and two neurotic cats, and his first volume of poetry, *They Were Called Records, Kids*, was released by MoonPath Press in 2018.

**Ina Roy-Faderman's** poetry has appeared in *Principium, Pigeon Papers, Trash Panda Haiku*, and other venues. A native Nebraskan of Bengali heritage, she teaches biomedical ethics and serves as an assistant editor at *Right Hand Pointing*.

**Michael Scholtes** is a software engineer living in Ashland, Oregon.

**Amy Schrader** is the author of *The Plagiarist* (Finishing Line Press, 2017) and *The Situation & What Crosses It* (MoonPath Press, 2014). She writes sonnets and works as an accountant in Seattle, Washington.

**Randolph Douglas Schuder** works as a fine art model in the Seattle area. In 2000, Rose Alley Press published his collection, *To Enter the Stillness*. His poems also appear in all three Rose Alley Press anthologies. His interests include mushroom foraging, day hiking and backpacking, and, not least, fly-fishing.

**Judith Shapiro** spends half the year on the opposite coast, marveling at the sun that sets over the ocean instead of rising. When the novel she's writing looks the other way, she secretly writes anything else. Her work appears in *The Citron Review, Moss Piglet, The Sun,* and elsewhere. PeaceInEveryLeaf.com.

**David Sheskin's** work has been published in numerous magazines over the years. Most recently his work has appeared in *The Dalhousie Review, The Satirist, Shenandoah,* and *Chicago Quarterly Review*. His most recent books are *David Sheskin's Cabinet of Curiosities* and *Outrageous Wedding Announcements*.

**Martha Silano's** most recent collection is *Gravity Assist* (Saturnalia Books, 2019). Previous collections include *Reckless Lovely* and *The Little Office of the Immaculate Conception*, also from Saturnalia Books. Martha's poems have appeared in *Poetry* and *American Poetry Review*, among others. She teaches at Bellevue College. Learn more at marthasilano.net.

**Judith Skillman's** poems have appeared in *Commonweal, Threepenny Review, ZYZZYVA,* and other literary journals. She has received awards from Academy of American Poets and Artist Trust. *Oscar the Misanthropist* won the 2021 Floating Bridge Press Chapbook Award. Judith's new collection is *Subterranean Address*, Deerbrook Editions. Visit www.judithskillman.com.

**Peter Gregg Slater**, a historian, has taught at several institutions, including Dartmouth College and the University of California, Berkeley. In retirement, he has devoted himself to creative writing. His poetry, fiction, parody, and essays have appeared in *DASH, Workers Write!, The Satirist, Masque & Spectacle*, and *The Westchester Review*.

**Michael Spence** drove public-transit buses in the Seattle area for thirty years. His poems have appeared recently or are forthcoming in *Atlanta Review, The Hudson Review, The New Criterion, Rattle, The Southern Review*, and *Tar River Poetry*. His latest book, *Umbilical* (St. Augustine's Press, 2016), won *The New Criterion* Poetry Prize.

**Joannie Stangeland** is the author of several poetry collections, most recently *The Scene You See*. Her poems have also appeared in *The MacGuffin, Two Hawks Quarterly, Prairie Schooner, New England Review*, and other journals. Joannie holds an MFA from the Rainier Writing Workshop.

**Timothy Steele's** collections of verse include *Toward the Winter Solstice; The Color Wheel*; and *Sapphics and Uncertainties*. He has also published two prose books about poetry—*Missing Measures* and *All the Fun's in How You Say a Thing*—and has edited *The Poems of J. V. Cunningham*.

**Diane Stone**, a former technical writer-editor, lives on Whidbey Island, north of Seattle. Her work has been published in *Crosswinds Poetry Journal, The Comstock Review, The Main Street Rag, Minerva Rising, Chautauqua*, and elsewhere. A book of poetry, *Small Favors* (Kelsay Books), was published in 2021.

**Doug Stone** lives in Albany, Oregon. He has written three collections of poetry: *The Season of Distress and Clarity, The Moon's Soul Shimmering on the Water*, and *Sitting in Powell's Watching Burnside Dissolve in Rain*.

**Stuart Stromin** is an award-winning South African-American writer and filmmaker living in Los Angeles. He was educated at Rhodes University, South Africa; the Alliance Française de Paris; and UCLA.

**Jean Syed** is from Lancashire, England; attended Birmingham University; and worked in Portsmouth and the East Midlands. Her poems have appeared in *The Lyric, The Raintown Review, The Journal of Formal Poetry, Lighten Up Online*, and other journals. Her chapbooks are *Sonnets* (Dos Madres Press) and *My Portfolio* (Kelsay Books).

**Alarie Tennille** was a pioneer coed at the University of Virginia, where she earned her degree in English, Phi Beta Kappa key, and a black belt in Feminism. Art, family, quirky news, and cats are her chief muses. *The Ekphrastic Review* (online) is her home away from home.

**Richard Wakefield** taught humanities at Tacoma Community College for forty-four years. His first poetry collection, *East of Early Winters*, won the Richard Wilbur Award, and his second collection, *A Vertical Mile*, was shortlisted for the Poets' Prize. His latest, *Terminal Park*, was published by Able Muse in 2022.

**Cody Walker** is the author of several poetry collections, including *The Self-Styled No-Child* (Waywiser, 2016). His work appears in *The New York Times Magazine* and *The Best American Poetry*. He directs the Bear River Writers' Conference and lives in Ann Arbor with three people and an orange tabby.

**Diane Webster's** goal is to remain open to poetry ideas in everyday life, nature, or an overheard phrase. Diane enjoys the challenge of transforming images into words to fit her poems. Her work has appeared in *El Portal, North Dakota Quarterly, New English Review,* and other literary magazines.

**Gail White** is a formalist poet whose totem animal is the cat, as evidenced by her chapbook of cat poetry, *Catechism*. She lives in Breaux Bridge, Louisiana, where she currently owns two cats and feeds three others.

**Griffith Williams** is a poet and printer based in Kenmore, Washington.

**Deborah Woodard** is a poet, translator, and teacher living in Seattle, Washington.

Henriëtte Ronner-Knip, *The Globetrotters*

# ABOUT OUR CONTRIBUTING ARTISTS

Poet **Ronda Piszk Broatch** is also a photographer and graphic artist in a parallel dimension. Her photographs and digital art pieces have graced the covers of several poetry collections, including her own two books from MoonPath Press, *Chaos Theory For Beginners* (2023) and *Lake of Fallen Constellations* (2015).

*Cat on a Roof*: used by permission of the artist

**Caroline Ellen Clark**, BFA, MAT, is a visual arts educator with a masters in teaching and graphic arts. She's taught in public and private schools and done private art tutoring. Current project: utilizing her recent UX certificate (from UW) and illustrating some children books. Caroline lives in Bellevue, Washington.

*Crouching Cat*: used by permission of the artist

**Deborah DeWit** (cover art) has been a working artist for over 45 years. Everyday life and her interest in ideas and beauty are the subjects of her artwork. She currently lives, works and exhibits her paintings on the North Oregon Coast—and in her life has known and loved many cats. Visit her online at Huckleberry Studios: www.deborahdewit.com.

Cover art: *Wisdom and Wildness*. Pastel, 20"x30", 2006, used by permission of the artist.

**Jean Bernard Duvivier** (1775–1833) was certainly a cat lover. A deft artist and draftsman he sketched many cats, most probably his own, using charcoal and colored crayons.

*Liggende kat*: jenikirbyhistory.getarchive.net

**Tachibana Morikuni** (1679–1748) was a painter and printmaker active in Osaka, Japan. He studied under Tsuruzawa Tanzan.

*Domestic cat nursing kittens*: Wikimedia Commons

**Pierre-Auguste Renoir** (1841–1919) was a French artist who was a leading painter in the Impressionist style. As a celebrator of beauty and especially feminine sensuality, Herbert Read wrote that "Renoir is the final representative of a tradition which runs directly from Rubens to Watteau."

*Woman with a Cat*: National Gallery of Art (nga.gov)

**Henriëtte Ronner-Knip** (1821–1909) was a Dutch-Belgian artist chiefly in the Romantic style who is best known for her animal paintings; especially cats.

*Curiosity, De Pianoles door, en her Katjes, The Globetrotters, Katjesspel, Naschkätzchen, Primer Part II, St. Nicholas series*: Wikimedia Commons

**Félix Vallotton** (1865–1925) was a Swiss and French painter and printmaker associated with the group of artists known as Les Nabis. He was an important figure in the development of the modern woodcut.

*Ex-Libris L. Joly, La Flûte, La Paresse*: Wikimedia Commons

**Jean-Antoine Watteau** (1684–1721) was a French painter and draughtsman whose brief career spurred the revival of interest in color and movement, as seen in the tradition of Correggio and Rubens.

*Jéune leopard s'étirant*: Wikimedia Commons

Henriëtte Ronner-Knip, *St. Nicholas series*

# INDEX OF CONTRIBUTING ARTISTS AND POETS

Félix Vallotton, *La Flûte*

Made in the USA
Monee, IL
10 January 2024

50634520R00144